Gledhill Shaw Cooperative Personnel Services CPS Prep

Gledhill Shaw Cooperative Personnel Services (CPS) test and Occupational Skills (OS) Assessment Study Guide with Practice Questions

Copyright © 2025 Complete Test Preparation Inc. ALL RIGHTS RESERVED. No part of this book may be reproduced or transferred in any form or by any means, graphic, electronic, or mechanical, including photocopying, recording, web distribution, taping, or by any information storage retrieval system, without the written permission of the author.

Notice: Complete Test Preparation Inc. makes every reasonable effort to obtain from reliable sources accurate, complete, and timely information about the tests covered in this book. Nevertheless, changes can be made in the tests or the administration of the tests at any time and Complete Test Preparation Inc. makes no representation or warranty, either expressed or implied as to the accuracy, timeliness, or completeness of the information contained in this book. Complete Test Preparation Inc. makes no representations or warranties of any kind, express or implied, about the completeness, accuracy, reliability, suitability or availability with respect to the information contained in this document for any purpose. Any reliance you place on such information is therefore strictly at your own risk.

The author(s) shall not be liable for any loss incurred as a consequence of the use and application, directly or indirectly, of any information presented in this work. Sold with the understanding, the author(s) is not engaged in rendering professional services or advice. If advice or expert assistance is required, the services of a competent professional should be sought.

The company, product and service names used in this publication are for identification purposes only. All trademarks and registered trademarks are the property of their respective owners. Complete Test Preparation Inc. is not affiliated with any educational institution.

We strongly recommend that students check with exam providers for up-to-date information regarding test content.

Published by

Complete Test Preparation Inc.
Victoria BC Canada
Visit us on the web at https://www.test-preparation.ca
Printed in the USA

ISBN: 9781772454604

Version 9 February 2025

About Complete Test Preparation Inc.

Why Us?
The Complete Test Preparation Team has been publishing high quality study materials since 2005, with a catalog of over 180 titles, in English, French, Spanish and Chinese, as well as ESL curriculum for all levels.

To keep up with the industry changes, we update everything all the time!

And the best part?
With every purchase, you're helping people all over the world improve themselves and their education. So thank you in advance for supporting this mission with us! Together, we are truly making a difference in the lives of those often forgotten by the system.

Charities that we support
https://www.test-preparation.ca/charities-and-non-profits/

You have definitely come to the right place.
If you want to spend your valuable study time where it will help you the most - we've got you covered today and tomorrow.

https://www.test-preparation.ca

Contents

6 Getting Started
    How this study guide is organized   7
    The Gledhill Shaw CPS Study Plan   7
    Making a Study Schedule   8

14 Reading and Listening
    Reading Comprehension Self Assessment   15
    Answer Key   31
    Help with Reading Comprehension   36
    Main Idea and Supporting Details   39
    Drawing Inferences And Conclusions   43
    Listening Self Assessment   47
    Answer Key   54
    Listening Tips and Tricks   55

57 Mathematics
    Mathematics Self Assessment   59
    Answer Key   67
    Basic Math Video Tutorials   71
    Fraction Tips, Tricks and Shortcuts   71
    Decimal Tips, Tricks and Shortcuts   77
    Percent Tips, Tricks and Shortcuts   78
    How to Answer Basic Math Multiple Choice   80
    How to Solve Word Problems   85
    Types of Word Problems   88

97 Mechanical Comprehension
    Mechanical Comprehension Self Assessment   99
    Answer Key   105
    Mechanical Comprehension Tutorials   107
    Gears and Gear Trains   110

112 People Situation Judgment
    Situation Judgment Self Assessment   115
    Answer Key   119

125 Mapping
    Mapping Self-Assessment   124
    Answer Key   129

130 Practice Test Questions Set 1
    Answer Key   193

215 Practice Test Questions Set 2
    Answer Key   274

295 After Taking a Practice Test
    What to do after you take a practice test   295
    Getting the Most from Practice Questions   295

297 Physical Fitness Requirements

299 Conclusion

301 Online Resources

Getting Started

CONGRATULATIONS! By deciding to take the Gledhill Shaw CPS exam, you have taken the first step toward a great future! Of course, there is no point in taking this important examination unless you intend to do your best to earn the highest grade you possibly can. That means getting yourself organized and discovering the best approaches, methods and strategies to master the material. Yes, that will require real effort and dedication, but if you are willing to focus your energy and devote the study time necessary, before you know it you will be opening that letter of acceptance to the firefighter service of your choice!

We know that taking on a new endeavour can be scary, and it is easy to feel unsure of where to begin. That's where we come in. This study guide is designed to help you improve your test-taking skills, show you a few tricks of the trade and increase both your competency and confidence.

The Gledhill Shaw CPS Test

The Gledhill Shaw CPS exam has five sections, reading comprehension, listening comprehension, basic math, mechanical aptitude and spatial perception.

While we seek to make our guide as comprehensive as possible, note that like all exams, the Gledhill Shaw CPS Exam might be adjusted at some future point. New material might be added, or content that is no longer relevant or applicable might be removed. It is always a good idea to give the materials you receive when you register to take the exam a careful review.

How this study guide is organized

This study guide is divided into three sections. The first section, self-assessments, which will help you recognize your areas of strength and weaknesses. This will be a boon when it comes to managing your study time most efficiently; there is not much point of focusing on material you have already got firmly under control. Instead, taking the self-assessments will show you where that time could be much better spent. In this area you will begin with a few questions to evaluate quickly your understanding of material that is likely to appear on the Gledhill Shaw CPS. If you do poorly in certain areas, simply work carefully through those sections in the tutorials and then try the self-assessment again.

The second section, Tutorials, offers information in each of the content areas, as well as strategies to help you master that material. The tutorials are not intended to be a complete course, but cover general principles. If you find that you do not understand the tutorials, it is recommended that you seek out additional instruction.

Third, we offer two sets of practice test questions, similar to those on the Gledhill Shaw CPS Exam.

The Gledhill Shaw CPS Study Plan

Now that you have made the decision to take the Gledhill Shaw, it is time to get started. Before you do another thing, you will need to figure out a plan of attack. The best study tip is to start early! The longer the time period you devote to regular study practice, the likelier you will be to retain the material and access it quickly. If you thought that 1 X 20 is the same as 2 x 10, guess what? It really is not, when it comes to study time. Reviewing material for just an hour per day over the course of 20 days is far better than studying for two hours a day for only 10 days. The more often you revisit a particular piece of information, the better you will know it. Not only will your grasp and understanding be better, but your ability to reach into your brain and quickly and efficiently pull out the tidbit you need, will be greatly enhanced as well.

The great Chinese scholar and philosopher Confucius believed that true knowledge could be defined as knowing what you know and what you do not know. The first step in preparing for the Gledhill Shaw test is to assess your strengths and weaknesses. You may already have an idea of what you know and what you do not know, but evaluating yourself using our Self- Assessment modules for each of the four areas, Reading, Language, Mathematics and Ability, will clarify the details.

Making a Study Schedule

To make your study time the most productive you will need to develop a study plan. The purpose of the plan is to organize all the bits of pieces of information in such a way that you will not feel overwhelmed. Rome was not built in a day, and learning everything you will need to know to pass the Gledhill Shaw test is going to take time, too. Arranging the material you need to learn into manageable chunks is the best way to go. Each study session should make you feel as though you have accomplished your goal, or at least are closer, and your goal is simply to learn what you planned to learn during that particular session. Try to organize the content in such a way that each study session builds on previous ones. That way, you will retain the information, be better able to access it, and review the previous bits and pieces at the same time.

Self-assessment

The Best Study Tip! The best study tip is to start early! The longer you study regularly, the more you will retain and 'learn' the material. Studying for 1 hour per day for 20 days is far better than studying for 2 hours for 10 days.

What don't you know?

The first step is to assess your strengths and weaknesses. You may already have an idea of where your weaknesses are, or you can take our Self-assessment modules for each of the content areas.

Exam Component	Rate 1 to 5
Reading Comprehension	
Listening comprehension	
Reading Comprehension	
Mathematics	
Basic Math & Arithmetic	
Word problems	
Geometry	
Mechanical Comprehension	
Mapping	
Situation Judgment	

Making a Study Schedule

The key to making a study plan is to divide the material you need to learn into manageable sized pieces and learn it, while at the same time reviewing the material that you already know.

Using the table above, any scores of 3 or below, you need to spend time learning, reviewing and practicing this subject area. A score of 4 means you need to review the material, but you don't have to spend time re-learning. A score of 5 and you are OK with just an occasional review before the exam.
A score of 0 or 1 means you really need to work on this should allocate the most time and the highest priority. Some students prefer a 5-day plan and others a 10-day plan. It also depends on how much time until the exam.

Here is an example of a 5-day plan based on an example from the table above:

Mechanical Comprehension: 1- Study 1 hour everyday – review on last day

Listening Comprehension: 4 - Review every second day

Geometry: 2 - Study 1 hour first day – then ½ hour everyday

Word problems: 5 - Review for ½ hour every other day

Reading Comprehension: 5 - Review for ½ hour every other day

Using this example, reading comprehension and word problems are good, and only need occasional review. Geometry is good and needs 'some' review. Listening comprehension needs a fair amount of work and Mechanical Comprehension is very weak and need the most time. Based on this, here is a sample study plan:

Day	Subject	Time
Monday		
Study	Mechanical Comp.	1 hour
Study	Geometry	1 hour
½ hour break		
Study	Listening Comp.	1 hour
Review	Reading Comp.	½ hour
Tuesday		
Study	Mechanical Comp.	1 hour
Study	Word Problems	½ hour
½ hour break		
Study	Geometry	½ hour
Review	Word Problems	½ hour
Review	Reading Comp.	½ hour
Wednesday		
Study	Mechanical Comp.	1 hour
Study	Word Problems	½ hour
½ hour break		
Study	Geometry	½ hour
Review	Reading Comp.	½ hour
Review	Listening Comp.	½ hour
Thursday		
Study	Mechanical Comp.	½ hour
Study	Word Problems	½ hour
Review	Geometry	½ hour
½ hour break		
Review	Reading Comp.	½ hour
Review	Word Problems	½ hour
Friday		
Review	Listening comprehension	½ hour
Review	Geometry	½ hour
½ hour break		
Review	Word Problems	½ hour
Review	Mechanical Comp.	½ hour

Using this example, adapt the study plan to your own schedule. This schedule assumes 2 ½ - 3 hours available to study everyday for a 5 day period.

First, write out what you need to study and how much. Next figure out how many days before the test. Note, do NOT study on the last day before the test. On the last day before the test, you won't learn anything and will probably only confuse yourself.

Make a table with the days before the test and the number of hours you have available to study each day. We suggest working with 1 hour and ½ hour time slots.

Start filling in the blanks, with the subjects you need to study the most, getting the most time, and the most regular time slots (i.e. everyday) and the subjects that you know getting the least time (e.g. ½ hour every other day, or every 3rd day).

Tips for making a schedule

Once you make a schedule, stick with it! Make your study sessions reasonable. If you make a study schedule and don't stick with it, you set yourself up for failure. Instead, schedule study sessions that are a bit shorter and set yourself up for success! Make sure your study sessions are do-able. Studying is hard work, but after you pass, you can party and take a break!

Schedule breaks. Breaks are just as important as study time. Work out a rotation of studying and breaks that works for you.

Build up study time. If you find it hard to sit still and study for 1 hour straight through, build up to it. Start with 20 minutes, and then take a break. Once you get used to 20-minute study sessions, increase the time to 30 minutes. Gradually work you way up to 1 hour.

40 minutes to 1 hour is optimal. Studying for longer than this is tiring and not productive. Studying for shorter isn't long enough to be productive.

Studying Math. Studying Math is different from studying other subjects because you use a different part of your brain. The best way to study math is to practice everyday. This will train your mind to think in a mathematical way. If you miss a day or days, the mathematical mind-set is gone and you have to start all over again to build it up.

More on how to study math
https://www.test-preparation.ca/study-math/

How to Study
For more information, see our How to Study Guide at
https://www.test-preparation.ca/learning-study/

Flash Cards - The Complete Guide

https://www.test-preparation.ca/flash-cards/

Using your Daily Routine to Study

https://www.test-preparation.ca/daily-routine/

Reading and Listening Comprehension

This section contains a self-assessment and reading comprehension tutorials. The tutorials are designed to familiarize general principles and the self-assessment contains general questions similar to the reading comprehension questions likely to be on the Gledhill Shaw, but are not intended to be identical to the exam questions, **and are intended for skill practice only**. The tutorials are not designed to be a complete reading comprehension course, and it is assumed that students have some familiarity with reading comprehension questions. If you do not understand parts of the tutorial, or find the questions or tutorials difficult, it is recommended that you seek out additional instruction.

Tour of the Gledhill Shaw Reading Comprehension Content

The Gledhill Shaw reading comprehension section has 30 reading comprehension questions. Below is a detailed list of the types of reading questions that generally appear on the Gledhill Shaw CPS test.

- Draw logical conclusions

- Make predictions

- Analyze passages to solve problems or identify sequences

- Vocabulary - Give the definition of a word from context

- Summarize

- Identify specific facts or details from a passage and distinguish facts and details.

One Firefighter tests (IMPA) have a logic section where you are asked to draw logical conclusions from a written passage. Logical reasoning questions are included here in the reading section.

The questions below are not the same as you will find on the Gledhill Shaw exam - that would be too easy! And nobody knows what the questions will be and they change all the time. Mostly the changes consist of substituting new questions for old, but the changes can be new question formats or styles, changes to the number of questions in each section, changes to the time limits for each section and combining sections. Below are general reading questions that cover the same areas as the Gledhill Shaw for skill practice. So, while the format and exact wording of the questions may differ slightly, and change from year to year, if you can answer the questions below, you will have no problem with the reading comprehension section of the Gledhill Shaw test.

Reading Comprehension Self Assessment

The purpose of the self-assessment is:

- Identify your strengths and weaknesses.

- Develop your personalized study plan (above)

- Get accustomed to the Gledhill Shaw test format

- Extra practice – the self-assessments are almost a full 3rd practice test!

- Provide a baseline score for preparing your study schedule.

Since this is a Self-assessment, and depending on how confident you are with Reading Comprehension, timing is optional. The Gledhill Shaw exams usually have about 30 reading questions. The self-assessment has 14 questions, so allow about 20 minutes to complete this assessment.

Once complete, use the table below to assess your understanding of the content, and prepare your study schedule described in chapter 1.

80% - 100%	Excellent – you have mastered the content
60 – 79%	Good. You have a working knowledge. Even though you can just pass this section, you may want to review the tutorials and do some extra practice to see if you can improve your mark.
40% - 59%	Below Average. You do not understand the reading comprehension problems. Review the tutorials, and retake this quiz again in a few days, before proceeding to the practice test questions.
Less than 40%	Poor. You have a very limited understanding of the reading comprehension problems. Please review the tutorials, and retake this quiz again in a few days, before proceeding to the practice test questions.

Reading Comprehension Self-Assessment

	A	B	C	D
1	○	○	○	○
2	○	○	○	○
3	○	○	○	○
4	○	○	○	○
5	○	○	○	○
6	○	○	○	○
7	○	○	○	○
8	○	○	○	○
9	○	○	○	○
10	○	○	○	○
11	○	○	○	○
12	○	○	○	○
13	○	○	○	○
14	○	○	○	○
15	○	○	○	○
16	○	○	○	○

Questions 1 – 4 refer to the following passage.

Passage 1 - Who Was Anne Frank?

You may have heard mention of the word Holocaust in your History or English classes. The Holocaust took place from 1939-1945. It was an attempt by the Nazi party to purify the human race, by eliminating Jews, Gypsies, Catholics, homosexuals and others they deemed inferior to their "perfect" Aryan race. The Nazis used Concentration Camps, which were sometimes used as Death Camps, to exterminate the people they held in the camps. The saddest fact about the Holocaust was the over one million children under the age of sixteen died in a Nazi concentration camp. Just a few weeks before World War II was over, Anne Frank was one of those children to die.

Before the Nazi party began its persecution of the Jews, Anne Frank had a happy live. She was born in June of 1929. In June of 1942, for her 13th birthday, she was given a simple present which would go onto impact the lives of millions of people around the world. That gift was a small red diary that she called Kitty. This diary was to become Anne's most treasured possession when she and her family hid from the Nazi's in a secret annex above her father's office building in Amsterdam.

For 25 months, Anne, her sister Margot, her parents, another family, and an elderly Jewish dentist hid from the Nazis in this tiny annex. They were never permitted to go outside, and their food and supplies were brought to them by Miep Gies and her husband, who did not believe in the Nazi persecution of the Jews. It was a very difficult life for young Anne and she used Kitty as an outlet to describe her life in hiding. After 2 years, Anne and her family were betrayed and arrested by the Nazis. To this day, nobody is exactly sure who betrayed the Frank family and the other annex residents. Anne, her mother, and her sister were separated from Otto Frank, Anne's father. Then, Anne and Margot were separated from their mother. In March of 1945, Margot Frank died of starvation in a Concentration Camp. A few days later, at the age of 15, Anne Frank died of typhus. Of all the people who hid in the Annex, only Otto Frank survived the Holocaust.

Otto Frank returned to the Annex after World War II. It was there that he found Kitty, filled with Anne's thoughts and feelings about being a persecuted Jewish girl. Otto Frank had Anne's diary published in 1947 and it has remained continuously in print ever since. Today, the diary has been published in over 55 languages and more than 24 million copies have been sold around the world. The Diary of Anne Frank tells the story of a brave young woman who tried to see the good in all people.

1. From the context clues in the passage, what does annex mean?

    a. Attic

    b. Bedroom

    c. Basement

    d. Kitchen

2. Why do you think Anne's diary has been published in 55 languages?

    a. So everyone could understand it.

    b. So people around the world could learn more about the horrors of the Holocaust.

    c. Because Anne was Jewish but hid in Amsterdam and died in Germany.

    d. Because Otto Frank spoke many languages.

3. From the description of Anne and Margot's deaths in the passage, what can we assume typhus is?

    a. The same as starving to death.

    b. An infection the Germans gave to Anne.

    c. A disease Anne caught in the concentration camp.

    d. Poison gas used by the Germans to kill Anne.

4. In the third paragraph, what does outlet mean?

   a. A place to plug things into the wall

   b. A store where Miep bought cheap supplies for the Frank family

   c. A hiding space similar to an Annex

   d. A place where Anne could express her private thoughts.

Questions 5 – 8 refer to the following passage.

Passage 2 - Was Dr. Seuss A Real Doctor?

A favorite author for over 100 years, Theodor Seuss Geisel was born on March 2, 1902. Today, we celebrate the birthday of the famous "Dr. Seuss" by hosting Read Across America events throughout the March. School children around the country celebrate the "Doctor's" birthday by making hats, giving presentations and holding read aloud circles featuring some of Dr. Seuss' most famous books.

But who was Dr. Seuss? Did he go to medical school? Where was his office? You may be surprised to know that Theodor Seuss Geisel was not a medical doctor at all. He took on the nickname Dr. Seuss when he became a noted children's book author. He earned the nickname because people said his books were "as good as medicine." All these years later, his nickname has lasted and he is known as Dr. Seuss all across the world.

Think back to when you were a young child. Did you ever want to try "green eggs and ham?" Did you try to "Hop on Pop?" Do you remember learning about the environment from a creature called The Lorax? Of course, you must recall one of Seuss' most famous characters; that green Grinch who stole Christmas. These stories were all written by Dr. Seuss and featured his signature rhyming words and letters. They also featured made up words to enhance his rhyme scheme and even though many of his characters were made up, they sure seem real to us today.

And what of his "signature" book, The Cat in the Hat? You must remember that cat and Thing One and Thing Two from your childhood. Did you know that in the early 1950's there was a growing concern in America that children were not becoming avid readers? This was, book publishers thought, because children found books dull and uninteresting. An intelligent publisher sent Dr. Seuss a book of words that he thought all children should learn as young readers. Dr. Seuss wrote his famous story The Cat in the Hat, using those words. We can see, over the decades, just how much influence his writing has had on very young children. That is why we celebrate this doctor's birthday each March.

5. What does the word "avid" mean in the last paragraph?

    a. Good

    b. Interested

    c. Slow

    d. Fast

6. What can we infer from the statement " His books were like medicine?"

    a. His books made people feel better

    b. His books were in doctor's office waiting rooms

    c. His books took away fevers

    d. His books left a funny taste in readers' mouths.

7. Why is the publisher in the last paragraph called "intelligent?"

    a. The publisher knew how to read.

    b. The publisher knew that kids did not like to read.

    c. The publisher knew Dr. Seuss would be able to create a book that sold well.

    d. The publisher knew that Dr. Seuss would be able to write a book that would get young children interested in reading.

8. The theme of this passage is

   a. Dr. Seuss was not a doctor.

   b. Dr. Seuss influenced the lives of generations of young children.

   c. Dr. Seuss wrote rhyming books.

   d. Dr. Seuss' birthday is a good day to read a book.

Questions 9 - 11 refer to the following passage.

Keeping Tropical Fish

Keeping tropical fish at home or in your office used to be very popular. Today, interest has declined, but it remains as rewarding and relaxing a hobby as ever. Ask any tropical fish hobbyist, and you will hear how soothing and relaxing watching colorful fish live their lives in the aquarium. If you are considering keeping tropical fish as pets, here is a list of the basic equipment you will need.

A filter is essential for keeping your aquarium clean and your fish alive and healthy. There are different types and sizes of filters and the right size for you depends on the size of the aquarium and the level of stocking. Generally, you need a filter with a 3 to 5 times turn over rate per hour. This means that the water in the tank should go through the filter about 3 to 5 times per hour.

Most tropical fish do well in water temperatures ranging between 24^0 C and 26^0 C, though each has its own ideal water temperature. A heater with a thermostat is necessary to regulate the water temperature. Some heaters are submersible and others are not, so check carefully before you buy.

Lights are also necessary, and come in a large variety of types, strengths and sizes. A light source is necessary for plants in the tank to photosynthesize and give the tank a more attractive appearance. Even if you plan to use plastic plants, the fish still require light, although here you can use a lower strength light source.

A hood is necessary to keep dust, dirt and unwanted materials out of the tank. Sometimes the hood can also help prevent evaporation. Another requirement is aquarium gravel. This will improve the aesthetics of the aquarium and is necessary if you plan to have real plants.

9. What is the general tone of this article?

   a. Formal
   b. Informal
   c. Technical
   d. Opinion

10. Which of the following cannot be inferred?

   a. Gravel is good for aquarium plants.
   b. Fewer people have aquariums in their office than at home.
   c. The larger the tank, the larger the filter required.
   d. None of the above.

11. What evidence does the author provide to support their claim that aquarium lights are necessary?

   a. Plants require light.
   b. Fish and plants require light.
   c. The author does not provide evidence for this statement.
   d. Aquarium lights make the aquarium more attractive.

12. Which of the following is an opinion?

   a. Filter with a 3 to 5 times turn over rate per hour are required.

   b. Aquarium gravel improves the aesthetics of the aquarium.

   c. An aquarium hood keeps dust, dirt and unwanted materials out of the tank.

   d. Each type of tropical fish has its own ideal water temperature.

Questions 13 - 16 refer to the following passage.

The Civil War

The Civil War began on April 12, 1861. The first shots of the Civil War were fired in Fort Sumter, South Carolina. Even though more American lives were lost in the Civil War than in any other war, not one person died on that first day. The war began because eleven Southern states seceded from the Union and tried to start their own government, The Confederate States of America.

Why did the states secede? The issue of slavery was a primary cause of the Civil War. The eleven southern states relied heavily on their slaves to foster their farming and plantation lifestyles. The northern states, many of whom had already abolished slavery, did not think that the southern states should have slaves. The north wanted to free all the slaves and President Lincoln's goal was to both end slavery and preserve the Union. He had Congress declare war on the Confederacy on April 14, 1862. For four long, blood soaked years, the North and South fought.

From 1861 to mid 1863, it seemed as if the South would win this war. However, on July 1, 1863, an epic three day battle was waged on a field in Gettysburg, Pennsylvania. Gettysburg is remembered for being the bloodiest battle in American history. At the end of the three days, the North turned the tide of the war in their favor. The North then went on to dominate the South for the remainder of the war. Another famous event is General Sherman's "March to The Sea," where he famously led the Union Army through Georgia and the Carolinas, burning and destroying everything in their path.

In 1865, the Union army invaded and captured the Confederate capital of Richmond Virginia. Robert E. Lee, leader of the Confederacy surrendered to General Ulysses S. Grant, leader of the Union forces, on April 9, 1865. The Civil War was over and the Union was preserved.

13. What does secede mean?

    a. To break away from

    b. To accomplish

    c. To join

    d. To lose

14. Which of the following statements summarizes a FACT from the passage?

    a. Congress declared war and then the Battle of Fort Sumter began.

    b. Congress declared war after shots were fired at Fort Sumter.

    c. President Lincoln was pro slavery

    d. President Lincoln was at Fort Sumter with Congress

15. Which event finally led the Confederacy to surrender?

    a. The battle of Gettysburg

    b. The battle of Bull Run

    c. The invasion of the confederate capital of Richmond

    d. Sherman's March to the Sea

16. What does the word abolish as used in this passage mean?

   a. To ban
   b. To polish
   c. To support
   d. To destroy

17. What does a table primarily help to organize?

   a. Text data
   b. Quantitative and qualitative data
   c. Images and graphics
   d. Audio data

18. In a table, what does the term 'header' refer to?

   a. The first row
   b. The last row
   c. The first column
   d. The cells with numerical values

19. When interpreting a graph, what does the y-axis typically represent?

   a. Independent variable
   b. Dependent variable
   c. Categories
   d. Legend

20. Which of the following is a common type of diagram used to show relationships among various elements?

   a. Bar chart
   b. Venn diagram
   c. Pie chart
   d. Line graph

21. What is the purpose of a caption in relation to tables or graphs?

    a. To provide a title only
    b. To summarize the data
    c. To describe the source
    d. To explain the content and context

Questions 22 - 27 refer to the following table

Year	Sales (millions)	Profit (millions)	Employees
2020	50	10	200
2021	60	12	220
2022	70	14	240
2023	80	16	260
2024	90	18	280

22. What was the trend in the number of employees from 2020 to 2024?

    a. Decreasing
    b. Constant
    c. Increasing
    d. Fluctuating

23. What was the average profit per year from 2020 to 2024?

    a. 12 million
    b. 14 million
    c. 16 million
    d. 18 million

24. How much did the sales increase from 2020 to 2024?

    a. 30%
    b. 40%
    c. 50%
    d. 80%

25. What was the percentage increase in the number of employees from 2020 to 2024?

    a. 20%
    b. 30%
    c. 40%
    d. 50%

26. If the trend continues, what would be the expected sales in 2025?

    a. 95 million
    b. 100 million
    c. 105 million
    d. 110 million

27. What is the ratio of profit to sales in 2023?

    a. 1:5
    b. 1:4
    c. 1:3
    d. 1:2

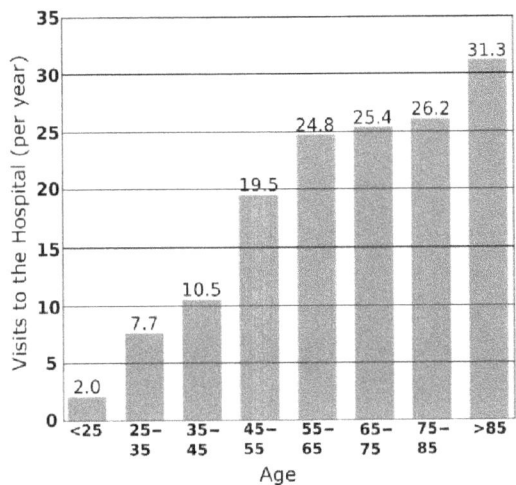

28. Consider the graph above.

How many hospital visits per year does a person aged 85 or more make?

a. 26.2
b. 31.3
c. More than 31.3
d. A decision cannot be made from this graph.

29. Based on this graph, how many visits per year do you expect a person that is 95 or older to make?

a. More than 31.3
b. Less than 31.3
c. 31.3
d. A decision cannot be made from this graph.

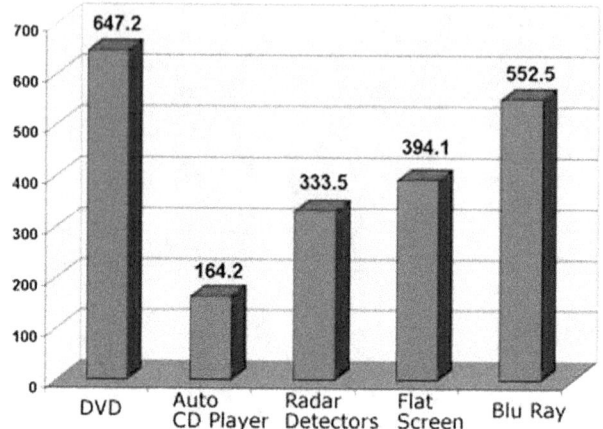

**30. Consider the graph above.
What is the third best-selling product?**

    a. Radar Detectors

    b. Flat Screen

    c. Blu Ray

    d. Auto CD Players

Answer Key

1. A
We know that an annex is like an attic because the text states the annex was above Otto Frank's building.

Choice B is incorrect because an office building doesn't have bedrooms. Choice C is incorrect because a basement would be below the office building. Choice D is incorrect because there would not be a kitchen in an office building.

2. B
The diary has been published in 55 languages so people all over the world can learn about Anne. That is why the passage says it has been continuously in print.

Choice A is incorrect because it is too vague. Choice C is incorrect because it was published after Anne died and she did not write in all three languages. Choice D is incorrect because the passage does not give us any information about what languages Otto Frank spoke.

3. C
Use the process of elimination to figure this out.

Choice A cannot be the correct answer because, otherwise the passage would have simply said that Anne and Margot both died of starvation. Choices B and D cannot be correct because, if the Germans had done something specifically to murder Anne, the passage would have stated that directly. By the process of elimination, choice C has to be the correct answer.

4. D
We can figure this out using context clues. The paragraph is talking about Anne's diary and so, outlet in this instance is a place where Anne can pour her feelings.

Choice A is incorrect answer. That is the literal meaning of the word outlet and the passage is using the figurative meaning. Choice B is incorrect because that is the secondary literal meaning of the word outlet, as in an outlet mall. Again, we are looking for figurative meaning. Choice C is incorrect because there are no clues in the text to support that answer.

5. B
When someone is avid about something that means they are highly interested in the subject. The context clues are dull and boring, because they define the opposite of avid.

6. A
The author is using a simile to compare the books to medicine. Medicine is what you take when you want to feel better. They are suggesting that if you want to feel good, they should read Dr. Seuss' books.

Choice B is incorrect because there is no mention of a doctor's office. Choice C is incorrect because it is using the literal meaning of medicine and the author is using medicine in a figurative way. Choice D is incorrect because it makes no sense. We know not to eat books.

7. D
The publisher is described as intelligent because he knew to get in touch with a famous author to develop a book that children would be interested in reading.

Choice A is incorrect because we can assume that all book publishers must know how to read. Choice B is incorrect because it says in the article that more than one publisher was concerned whether children liked to read. Choice C is incorrect because there is no mention in the article about how well The Cat in the Hat sold when it was first published.

8. B
The passage describes in detail how Dr. Seuss had a great effect on the lives of children through his writing. It names several of his books, tells how he helped children become avid readers and explains his style of writing.

Choice A is incorrect because that is just one single fact about the passage. Choice C is incorrect because that is just one single fact about the passage. Choice D is incorrect because that is just one single fact about the passage. Again, choice B is correct because it encompasses ALL the facts in the passage, not just one single fact.

9. B
The general tone is informal.

10. B
The statement, "Fewer people have aquariums in their office than at home," cannot be inferred from this article.

11. B
Light is necessary for the fish and plants.

12. B
The following statement is an opinion, " Aquarium gravel improves the aesthetics of the aquarium."

13. A
Secede means to break away from because the 11 states wanted to leave the United States and form their own country.

Choice B is incorrect because the states were not accomplishing anything. Choice C is incorrect because the states were trying to leave the USA not join it. Choice D is incorrect because the states seceded before they lost the war.

14. B
Look at the dates in the passage. The shots were fired on April 12 and Congress declared war on April 14.

Choice C is incorrect because the passage states that Lincoln was against slavery. Choice D is incorrect because it never mentions who was or was not at Fort Sumter.

15. C
The passage states that Lee surrendered to Grant after the capture of the capital of the Confederacy, which is Richmond.

Choice A is incorrect because the war continued for 2 years after Gettysburg. Choice B is incorrect because that battle is not mentioned in the passage. Choice D is incorrect because the capture of the capital occurred after the march to the sea.

16. A
When the passage said that the North had *abolished* slavery, it implies that slaves were no longer allowed in the North. In essence slavery was banned.

Choice B makes no sense relative to the context of the passage. Choice C is incorrect because we know the North was fighting slavery, not for it. Choice D is incorrect because slavery is not a tangible thing that can be destroyed. It is a practice that had to be outlawed or banned.

17. B
A table helps to organize both quantitative and qualitative data in a structured format, making it easier to compare and analyze.

18. A
The header usually refers to the first row of a table that contains labels describing the contents of each column.

19. B
In most graphs, the y-axis represents the dependent variable, which is the outcome being measured and observed in relation to the independent variable on the x-axis.

20. B
A Venn diagram is commonly used to illustrate the relationships and intersections between different sets or categories.

21. C
A caption serves to explain the content and context of a table or graph, allowing readers to understand the significance of the data presented.

22. C
The number of employees increased each year from 2020 to 2024.

23. B
The average profit per year from 2020 to 2024 is calculated as (10 + 12 + 14 + 16 + 18) / 5 = 14 million.

24. D
Sales increased from 50 million in 2020 to 90 million in 2024, which is an increase of 40 million which is 80%
90 - 50 = 40 million increase in sales, so what percent is 50, is 40?

40/50 = x/100 solve for X
(40 X 100)/50 = 80

25. C
The number of employees increased from 200 in 2020 to 280 in 2024, which is a 40% increase ((280 - 200) / 200 * 100).

26. B
If the trend of increasing sales by 10 million per year continues, the expected sales in 2025 would be 90 million + 10 million = 100 million.

27. A
The ratio of profit to sales in 2023 is 16 million profit to 80 million sales, which simplifies to 1:5.

28. A
Based on this graph, a person that is 85 will make 26.2 visits to the hospital every year.

29. C
A person aged 95 or older would make more than 31.3 visits.

30. B
Flat Screen TVs are the third best-selling product.

Help with Reading Comprehension

At first sight, reading comprehension tests look challenging especially if you are given long essays to answer only two to three questions. While reading, you might notice your attention wandering, or you may feel sleepy. Do not be discouraged because there are various tactics and long range strategies that make comprehending even long, boring essays easier.

Your friends before your foes. It is always best to start with essays or passages with familiar subjects rather than those with unfamiliar ones. This approach applies the same logic as tackling easy questions before hard ones. Skip passages that do not interest you and leave them for later, when there is more time.

Don't use 'special' reading techniques. This is not the time for speed-reading or anything like that – just plain ordinary reading – not too slow and not too fast.

Read through the entire passage and the questions before you do anything. Many students try reading the questions first and then looking for answers in the passage thinking this approach is more efficient. What these students do not realize is that it is often hard to navigate in unfamiliar roads. If you do not familiarize yourself with the passage first, looking for answers become not only time-consuming but also dangerous because you might miss the context of the answer you are looking for. If you read the questions first you will only confuse yourself and lose valuable time.

Familiarize yourself with reading comprehension questions. If you are familiar with the common types of reading questions, you are able to take note of important parts of the passage, saving time. There are six major kinds of reading questions.

- **Main Idea**- Questions that ask for the central thought or significance of the passage.

- **Specific Details** - Questions that asks for explicitly stated ideas.

- **Drawing Inferences** - Questions that ask for a statement's intended meaning.

- **Tone or Attitude** - Questions that test your ability to sense the emotional state of the author.

- **Context Meaning** – Questions that ask for the meaning of a word depending on the context.

- **Technique** – Questions that ask for the method of organization or the writing style of the author.

Read. Read. Read. The best preparation for reading comprehension tests is always to read, read and read. If you are not used to reading lengthy passages, you will probably lose concentration. Increase your attention span by making a habit out of reading.

Reading Comprehension tests become less daunting when you have trained yourself to read and understand fast. Always remember that it is easier to understand passages you are interested in. Do not read through passages hastily. Make mental notes of ideas you may be asked.

Reading Strategy

When facing the reading comprehension section of a standardized test, you need a strategy to be successful. You want to keep several steps in mind:

- **First, make a note of the time and the number of sections**. Time your work accordingly. Typically, four to five minutes per section is sufficient. Second, read the directions for each selection thoroughly before beginning (and listen well to any additional verbal instructions, as they will often clarify obscure or confusing written guidelines). You must know exactly how to do what you're about to do!

- **Now you're ready to begin reading the selection.** Read the passage carefully, noting significant characters or events on a scratch sheet of paper or underlining on the test sheet. Many students find making a basic list in the margins helpful. Quickly jot down or underline one-word summaries of characters, notable happenings, numbers, or key ideas. This will help you better retain information and focus wandering thoughts. Remember, however, that your main goal in doing this is to find the information that answers the questions. Even if you find the passage interesting, remember your goal and work fast but stay on track.

- **Now read the question and all the choices.** Now you have read the passage, have a general idea of the main ideas, and have marked the important points. Read the question and all the choices. Never choose an answer without reading them all! Questions are often designed to confuse – stay focussed and clear. Usually the answer choices will focus on one or two facts or inferences from the passage. Keep these clear in your mind.

- **Search for the answer.** With a very general idea of what the different choices are, go back to the passage and scan for the relevant information. Watch for big words, unusual or unique words. These make your job easier as you can scan the text for the particular word.

- **Mark the Answer.** Now you have the key information the question is looking for. Go back to the question, quickly scan the choices and mark the correct one.

Understand and practice the different types of standardized reading comprehension tests. See the list above for the different types. Typically, there will be several questions dealing with facts from the selection, a couple more inference questions dealing with logical consequences of those facts, and periodically an application-oriented question surfaces to force you to make connections with what you already know. Some students prefer to answer the questions as listed, and feel classifying the question and then ordering is wasting precious time. Other students prefer to answer the different types of questions in order of how easy or difficult they are. The choice is yours and do whatever works for you. If you want to try answering in order of difficulty, here is a recommended order, answer fact questions first; they're easily found within the passage. Tackle inference problems next, after re-reading the question(s) as many times as you need to. Application or 'best guess' questions usually take the longest, so, save them for last.

Use the practice tests to try out both ways of answering and see what works for you.

For more help with reading comprehension, see Multiple Choice Secrets.
https://www.test-preparation.ca/multiple-choice-strategy/

Main Idea and Supporting Details

Identifying the main idea, topic and supporting details in a passage can feel like an overwhelming task. The passages used for standardized tests can be boring and seem difficult - Test writers don't use interesting passages or ones that talk about things most people are familiar with. Despite these obstacles, all passages and paragraphs will have the information you need to answer the questions.

The topic of a passage or paragraph is its subject. It's the general idea and can be summed up in a word or short phrase. On some standardized tests, there is a short description of the passage if it's taken from a longer work. Make sure you read the description as it might state the topic of the passage. If not, read the passage and ask yourself, "Who or what is this about?" For example:

Over the years, school uniforms have been hotly debated. Arguments are made that students have the right to show individuality and express themselves by choosing their own clothes. However, this brings up social and academic issues. Some kids cannot afford to wear the clothes they like and might be bullied by the "better dressed" students. With attention drawn to clothes and the individual, students will lose focus on class work and the reason they are in school. School uniforms should be mandatory.

Ask: What is this paragraph about?

Topic: school uniforms

Once you have the topic, it's easier to find the main idea. The main idea is a specific statement telling what the writer wants you to know about the topic. Writers usually state the main idea as a thesis statement. If you're looking for the main idea of a single paragraph, the main idea is called the topic sentence and will probably be the first or last sentence. If you're looking for the main idea of an entire passage, look for the thesis statement in either the first or last paragraph. The main idea is usually restated in the conclusion. To find the main idea of a passage or paragraph, follow these steps:

1. Find the topic.

2. Ask yourself, "What point is the author trying to make about the topic?"

3. Create your own sentence summarizing the author's point.

4. Look in the text for the sentence closest in meaning to yours.

Look at the example paragraph again. It's already established that the topic of the paragraph is school uniforms. What is the main idea/topic sentence?

Ask: "What point is the author trying to make about school uniforms?"

Summary: Students should wear school uniforms.

Topic sentence: School uniforms should be mandatory.

Main Idea: School uniforms should be mandatory.

Each paragraph offers supporting details to explain the main idea. The details could be facts or reasons, but they will always answer a question about the main idea. What? Where? Why? When? How? How much/many? Look at the example paragraph again. You'll notice that more than one sentence answers a question about the main idea. These are the supporting details.

Main Idea: School uniforms should be mandatory.

Ask: Why? Some kids cannot afford to wear clothes they like and could be bullied by the "better dressed" kids. Supporting Detail

With attention drawn to clothes and the individual, Students will lose focus on class work and the reason they are in school. Supporting Detail

What if the author doesn't state the main idea in a topic sentence? The passage will have an implied main idea. It's not as difficult to find as it might seem. Paragraphs are always organized around ideas. To find an implied main idea, you need to know the topic and then find the relationship between the supporting details. Ask yourself, "What is the point the author is making about the relationship between the details?"

Cocoa is what makes chocolate good for you. Chocolate comes in many varieties. These delectable flavors include milk chocolate, dark chocolate, semi-sweet, and white chocolate.

Ask: What is this paragraph about?

Topic: Chocolate

Ask: What? Where? Why? When? How? How much/many?

Supporting details: Chocolate is good for you because it is made of cocoa, Chocolate is delicious, Chocolate comes in different delicious flavors

Ask: What is the relationship between the details and what is the author's point?

Main Idea: Chocolate is good because it is healthy and it tastes good.

Testing Tips for Main Idea Questions

1. Skim the questions – not the answer choices - before reading the passage.

2. Questions about main idea might use the words "theme," "generalization," or "purpose."

3. Save questions about the main idea for last. Questions can often be found in order in the passage.

3. Underline topic sentences in the passage. Most tests allow you to write in your test booklet.

4. Answer the question in your own words before looking at the answer choices. Then match your answer with an answer choice.

5. Cross out incorrect answer choices immediately to prevent confusion.

6. If two of the answer choices mean the same thing but use different words, they are BOTH incorrect.

7. If a question asks about the whole passage, cross out the answer choices that apply only to part of it.

8. If only part of the information is correct, that answer choice is incorrect.

9. An answer choice that is too broad is incorrect. All information needs to be backed up by the passage.

10. Answer choices with extreme wording are usually incorrect.

Video Tutorial

https://www.test-preparation.ca/making-inferences/

Drawing Inferences And Conclusions (Logical Reasoning)

Drawing inferences and making conclusions happens all the time. In fact, you probably do it every time you read—sometimes without even realizing it! For example, remember the first time you saw the movie "The Lion King." When you meet Scar for the first time, he is trapping a helpless mouse with his sharp claws preparing to eat it. When you see this action you guess that Scar is going to be a bad character in the movie. Nothing appeared to tell you this. No caption came across the bottom of the screen that said "Bad Guy." No red arrow pointed to Scar and said "Evil Lion." No, you made an inference about his character based on the context clue you were given. You do the same thing when you read!

When you draw an inference or make a conclusion you are doing the same thing, you are making an educated guess based on the hints the author gives you. We call these hints "context clues." Scar trapping the innocent mouse is the context clue about Scar's character.

Usually you are making inferences and drawing conclusions the entire time that you are reading. Whether you realize it or not, you are constantly making educated guesses based on context clues. Think about a time you were reading a book and something happened that you were expecting to happen. You're not psychic! Actually, you were picking up on the context clues and making inferences about what was going to happen next!

Let's try an easy example. Read the following sentences and answer the questions at the end of the passage.

Shelly really likes to help people. She loves her job because she gets to help people every single day. However, Shelly has to work long hours and she can get called in the middle of the night for emergencies. She wears a white lab coat at work and usually she carries a stethoscope.

What is most likely Shelly's job?

    a. Musician

    b. Lawyer

    c. Doctor

    d. Teacher

This probably seemed easy. Drawing inferences isn't always this simple, but it is the same basic principle. How did you know Shelly was a doctor? She helps people, she works long hours, she wears a white lab coat, and she gets called in for emergencies at night. Context Clues! Nowhere in the paragraph did it say Shelly was a doctor, but you were able to draw that conclusion based on the information provided in the paragraph. This is how it's done!

There is a catch, though. Remember that when you draw inferences based on reading, you should only use the information given to you by the author. Sometimes it is easy for us to make conclusions based on knowledge that is already in our mind—but that can lead you to drawing an incorrect inference. For example, let's pretend there is a bully at your school named Brent. Now let's say you read a story and the main character's name is Brent. You could NOT infer that the character in the story is a bully just because his name is Brent. You should only use the information given to you by the author to avoid drawing the wrong conclusion.

Let's try another example. Read the passage below and answer the question.

Social media is an extremely popular new form of connecting and communicating over the internet. Since Facebook's original launch in 2004, millions of people have joined in the social media craze. In fact, it is estimated that almost 75% of all internet users aged 18 and older use some form of social media. Facebook started at Harvard University as a way to get students connected. However, it quickly grew into a worldwide phenomenon and today, the founder of Facebook, Mark Zuckerberg has an estimated net worth of 28.5 billion dollars.

Facebook is not the only social media platform, though. Other sites such as Twitter, Instagram, and Snapchat have since been invented and are quickly becoming just as popular! Many social media users actually use more than one type of social media. Furthermore, most social media sites have created mobile apps that allow people to connect via social media virtually anywhere in the world!

What likeliest reason that other social media sites like Twitter and Instagram were created?

 a. Professors at Harvard University made it a class project.

 b. Facebook was extremely popular and other people thought they could also be successful by designing social media sites.

 c. Facebook was not connecting enough people.

 d. Mark Zuckerberg paid people to invent new social media sites because he wanted lots of competition.

Here, the correct answer is B. Facebook was extremely popular and other people thought they could also be successful by designing social media sites. How do we know this? What are the context clues? Take a look at the first paragraph. What do we know based on this paragraph? Well, one sentence refers to Facebook's original launch. This suggests that Facebook was one of the first social media sites. In addition, we know that the founder of Facebook has been extremely successful and is worth billions of dollars. From this we can infer that other people wanted to imitate Facebook's idea and become just as successful as Mark Zuckerberg.

Let's go through the other answers. If you chose A, it might be because Facebook started at Harvard University, so you drew the conclusion that all other social media sites were also started at Harvard University. However, there is no mention of class projects, professors, or students designing social media. So there doesn't seem to be enough support for choice A.

If you chose C, you might have been drawing your own conclusions based on outside information. Maybe none of your friends are on Facebook, so you made an inference that Facebook didn't connect enough people, so more sites were invented. Or maybe you think the people who connect on Facebook are too old, so you don't think Facebook connects enough people your age. This might be true, but remember inferences should be drawn from the information the author gives you!

If you chose D, you might be using the information that Mark Zuckerberg is worth over 28 billion dollars. It would be easy for him to pay others to design new sites, but remember, you need to use context clues! He is very wealthy, but that statement was giving you information about how successful Facebook was—not suggesting that he paid others to design more sites!

So remember, drawing inferences and conclusions is simply about using the information you are given to make an educated guess. You do this every single day so don't let this concept scare you. Look for the context clues, make sure they support your claim, and you'll be able to make accurate inferences and conclusions!

Listening Comprehension Self-Assessment

	A	B	C	D
1	○	○	○	○
2	○	○	○	○
3	○	○	○	○
4	○	○	○	○
5	○	○	○	○
6	○	○	○	○
7	○	○	○	○
8	○	○	○	○
9	○	○	○	○
10	○	○	○	○
11	○	○	○	○
12	○	○	○	○
13	○	○	○	○
14	○	○	○	○
15	○	○	○	○

Directions: Scan the QR code below with any smartphone or tablet for an audio recording of the listening comprehension passages below. Or, have someone read them to you. Listen carefully to the passages and answer the questions that follow.

What is a QR Code?
A QR code looks like a barcode and it's used as a shortcut to link to content online using your phone's camera, saving you from typing lengthy addresses into your mobile browser.

Questions 1 - 4 refer to the following passage.

Passage 1 - Caterpillars

Butterflies and moths have a three stage life cycle. Caterpillars are the first or larval stage. Caterpillars can be either herbivores, feeding mostly on plants, or carnivores, feeding on other insects. Caterpillars eat continuously. Once they are too big for their body, they shed or molt their skin.

Some caterpillars have symbiotic relationships with other insects. A symbiotic relationship is where different species work together in a way that is either harmful or helpful. Symbiotic relationships are critical to many species and ecosystems.

Some caterpillars and ants have a symbiotic or mutual relationship where both benefit. Ants give some protection, and caterpillars provide the ants with honeydew nectar.

Ants and caterpillars communicate by vibrations through the soil as well as grunting and squeaking. Humans are not able to hear these communications.

Scan for audio or click
https://www.test-preparation.ca/audio/Caterpillar-2.mp3

1. What do most larvae spend their time doing?

    a. Eating

    b. Sleeping

    c. Communicating with ants.

    d. None of the above

2. Are all caterpillars herbivores?

    a. Yes

    b. No, some eat insects

3. What benefit do larvae get from association with ants?

    a. They do not receive any benefit.

    b. Ants give them protection.

    c. Ants give them food.

    d. Ants give them honeydew secretions.

4. Do ants or larvae benefit most from association?

    a. Ants benefit most

    b. Larvae benefit most

    c. Both benefit about the same

    d. Neither benefits

Questions 5 - 7 refer to the following passage.

Passage 2 - Fire

Fire is a chemical reaction producing light, flames, heat and generally smoke. This reaction is an example of rapid oxidation.

Other types of oxidation, such as rust or digestion occur very slowly in comparison.

The visible part of the chemical reaction, the flame, is different colors depending on the material burning. The flame is incandescent particles of soot. With more oxygen, the fire reaction is hotter and burns more cleanly, producing less soot, and the flame turns blue. Many fires burn at 1000 degrees Celsius (1800 Fahrenheit).

Scan for audio or click
https://www.test-preparation.ca/audio/Fire-2.mp3

5. Are oxidation processes like rust the same as fire?

   a. Yes
   b. No

6. What causes flames to have different colors?

    a. The heat of the fire

    b. The material burning

    c. Impurities in the surrounding air

    d. None of the above.

Questions 7 – 9 refer to the following passage.

Passage 3 - Gardens

Roman gardens were initially built to supply the household with vegetables and herbs. Later, the influence from Greek and Persian gardens changed Roman gardens to pleasure gardens in palaces and villas, as well as public parks meant for enjoyment and exercise. At this time Roman gardens had their famous statues and sculptures.

Later with the fall of the Roman Empire, gardening declined and during the Middle Ages, gardening was strictly for herbs used in various medicines, and for decorating churches.

Persian garden were surrounded by walls and meant to look like paradise. Traditional Islamic gardens are heavily influence by the desert, an important part of Persian culture. Therefore, water and shade are important elements. Gardens, in Islamic culture, are for meditation and rest. Sunlight is an important feature of Persian gardens and often the architecture, layout and textures highlight reflected sunlight. Persian gardens are built on an indoor/outdoor plan that often uses courtyards.

Scan for audio or click
https://www.test-preparation.ca/audio/Gardens-2.mp3

7. What is a characteristic feature of Roman gardens?

    a. Statues and Sculptures

    b. Flower beds

    c. Medicinal Herbs

    d. Courtyard gardens

8. When did gardening decline?

    a. Before the Fall of Rome.

    b. Gardening did not decline.

    c. Before the Middle Ages.

    d. After the Fall of Rome.

9. What kind of gardening was done during the Middle Ages?

    a. Gardening with hedges and vines

    b. Gardening with a wide variety of flowers

    c. Gardening for medicinal plants and decorating churches

    d. Gardening divided by watercourses

Questions 10 – 12 refer to the following passage.

Passage 4 - Insect Pests

A pest is an organism that is destructive to crops, humans, structures, or other animals. Insect pests make up about 1% of the insect family. Many insects such as bees and silkworms are beneficial.

Many blood-sucking insects carry diseases the pick up from infected hosts and pass on.

Some insects that were previously harmless, can become pests if they are introduced to a new area. In the new area often insects do not have natural predators.

Often insects carry diseases. The common housefly breeds on organic wastes and can carry diseases to food which is consumed by humans.

Pests can be controlled using insecticides and introducing natural predators. For example, farmers introduce predators such as ladybugs to their crops to control various insect pests.

Scan for audio or click
https://www.test-preparation.ca/audio/InsectPests-2.mp3

10. How do humans control insects?

    a. By training them

    b. Using insecticides and other techniques

    c. In many different ways

    d. Humans don't control insects

11. What are examples of beneficial insects?

    a. Cows and bats

    b. Bees and silkworms

    c. Caterpillars and ants

    d. None of the above

12. What percent of insects are pests?

    a. 5%

    b. 10%

    c. 1%

    d. 3%

Answer Key

1. A
Caterpillars spend most of their time eating.

2. B
Some caterpillars are herbivores, others eat other insects (carnivores).

3. B
From the passage, the ants provide some degree of protection.

4. C
The association is mutual so they both benefit.

5. B
Fire is an oxidation process but is much faster than rust or digestion.

6. B
Depending on the materials burning, the flame is a different color.

7. A
Roman gardens are known for their statues and sculptures.

8. D
After the fall of Rome, gardening declined.

9. C
From the passage, "during the Middle Ages, gardening was strictly for herbs used in various medicines, and for decorating churches."

10. B
The techniques for controlling insects is taken from the last paragraph.

11. B
Bees and silkworms are examples of beneficial insects.

12. C
1% of the insect family are pests.

Listening Comprehension Tips and Tricks

Listening Comprehension tests are a kind of standardized evaluations that have a spoken passage or conversation, followed by multiple-choice questions from the passage.

Tips to get through a Listening Comprehension Exam

These tests represent challenges very different from other kinds of test. On one hand, you can't read the question over and over and think about it. On the other hand, when you listening to the audio, you have no idea of what you will be asked, so you may feel forced to memorize every word you're hearing t be ready for any question. These aspects are considered troubles for most students, but they aren't really that problematic, you just have to learn how to use these aspects in your advantage.

Here are some tips to face a Listening Comprehension test and live to tell it:

1. Fight anxiety
When it comes to tests, anxiety is your greatest enemy. You need a calm mind to reflect on the questions. This is especially important in listening comprehension exams, where you have only one or two chances to listen to the text, so you must fully concentrate on what you're hearing. Anxiety makes it harder to concentrate in the task you have in hands. To fight anxiety you need to be calm and confident of your own knowledge. Don't concentrate on the difficulties, focus on your strengths and think about your future success. More on test anxiety

2. Prepare yourself
This is a must in every kind of test: you have to study and prepare! That's the only way to get a good grade. Set up a good studying routine, that includes a quiet place and the resources you'll need to study comfortably, as well as a study plan. How to make a study plan   Setting up a productive study space

The study routine for a listening comprehension test is a bit different, because you need to center your preparation on you listening abilities, which means that you will have to listen a lot of texts to practice. Listen to English TV, radio, online videos or whatever you can find. After listening to a short passage, think of questions that could be asked and answer them.

Another exercise is to take notes from an audio passage and try to identify the main idea.

3. Know your weaknesses

Everybody has areas where they have difficulties, this is normal. The thing is that you shouldn't leave these areas as blank spaces - take note and fight them! For example, if you have difficulties understanding the accent, practice by playing an audio while reading the content, this gives you the opportunity to note the words with difficult pronunciation. The main thing isn't identifying the problems, focus on finding the solution to those problems.

4. Focus on the meaning

Most people believe that the questions of a listening comprehension test are literary questions about the text. Some types of questions, such as those on the CELPIP®, do ask for specific facts from the text. However, most questions are meant to assess whether you are capable of understanding ideas and draw conclusions about what they heard.

This means that memorizing the text while listening is useless; if the test uses the tale of Sleeping Beauty, for example, no one is going to ask about how many pillows she used, the questions will be related to the context of the story and the ideas that it communicates, like for example, what is the real reason that the evil fairy bewitched Aurora. So, forget about using your concentration to memorize every detail, instead concentrate on fully understanding the content of the text and its context.

MATHEMATICS

THIS SECTION CONTAINS A SELF-ASSESSMENT AND MATH TUTORIALS. The tutorials are designed to familiarize general principles and the self-assessment contains general questions similar to the math questions likely to be on the firefighter exam, but are not intended to be identical to the exam questions. The tutorials are not designed to be a complete math course, and it is assumed that students have some familiarity with math. If you do not understand parts of the tutorial, or find the tutorial difficult, it is recommended that you seek out additional instruction.

Mathematics Self-assessment

Below is a Mathematics Self-assessment. The purpose of the self-assessment is:

- Identify your strengths and weaknesses.

- Develop your personalized study plan (above)

- Get accustomed to the format

- Extra practice – the self-assessments are almost a full 3rd practice test!

Since this is a Self-assessment, and depending on how confident you are with math, timing yourself is optional. The Gledhill Shaw exams include a math section that covers decimals, fractions, metric conversions, percentages and word problems. Most firefighter exams have 25 math questions. The self-assessment has 30 questions, so allow 30 minutes, one minute per question to complete this assessment.

The questions below are not the same as you will find on the firefighter exam - that would be too easy! And nobody knows what the questions will be and they change all the time. Below are general math questions that cover the same areas. So, while the format and exact wording of the questions may differ slightly, and change from year to year, if you can answer the questions below, you will have no problem with the math section.

The self-assessment is designed to give you a baseline score in the different areas covered. Here is a brief outline of how your score on the self-assessment relates to your understanding of the material.

75% - 100%	Excellent – you have mastered the content
50 – 75%	Good. You have a working knowledge. Even though you can just pass this section, you may want to review the tutorials and do some extra practice to see if you can improve your mark.
25% - 50%	Below Average. You do not understand the content. Review the tutorials, and retake this quiz again in a few days, before proceeding to the rest of the practice test questions.
Less than 25%	Poor. You have a very limited understanding. Please review the Tutorials, and retake this quiz again in a few days, before proceeding to the rest of the practice test questions.

Mathematics Self-Assessment

	A	B	C	D	E		A	B	C	D	E
1	○	○	○	○	○	21	○	○	○	○	○
2	○	○	○	○	○	22	○	○	○	○	○
3	○	○	○	○	○	23	○	○	○	○	○
4	○	○	○	○	○	24	○	○	○	○	○
5	○	○	○	○	○	25	○	○	○	○	○
6	○	○	○	○	○	26	○	○	○	○	○
7	○	○	○	○	○	27	○	○	○	○	○
8	○	○	○	○	○	28	○	○	○	○	○
9	○	○	○	○	○	29	○	○	○	○	○
10	○	○	○	○	○	30	○	○	○	○	○
11	○	○	○	○	○						
12	○	○	○	○	○						
13	○	○	○	○	○						
14	○	○	○	○	○						
15	○	○	○	○	○						
16	○	○	○	○	○						
17	○	○	○	○	○						
18	○	○	○	○	○						
19	○	○	○	○	○						
20	○	○	○	○	○						

Basic Math

1. 389 + 454 =

    a. 853
    b. 833
    c. 843
    d. 863

2. 9,177 + 7,204 =

    a. 16,4712
    b. 16,371
    c. 16,381
    d. 15,412

3. 643 - 587 =

    a. 56
    b. 66
    c. 46
    d. 55

4. 3,406 - 2,767 =

    a. 629
    b. 720
    c. 639
    d. 649

5. 149 × 7 =

    a. 1032

    b. 1043

    c. 1059

    d. 1063

6. 467 × 41 =

    a. 19,147

    b. 21,227

    c. 23,107

    d. 18,177

7. 491 ÷ 9 =

    a. 54 r5

    b. 56 r6

    c. 57 r5

    d. 51 r

Decimals, Fractions and Percent

8. A boy has 5 red balls, 3 white balls and 2 yellow balls. What percent of the balls are yellow?

    a. 2%

    b. 8%

    c. 20%

    d. 12%

9. Add 10% of 300 to 50% of 20

    a. 50%
    b. 40%
    c. 60%
    d. 45%

10. Convert 75% to a fraction.

    a. 2/100
    b. 75/100
    c. 3/4
    d. 4/7

11. Multiply 3 by 25% of 40

    a. 75
    b. 30
    c. 68
    d. 35

12. What is 10% of 30 multiplied by 75% of 200?

    a. 450
    b. 750
    c. 20
    d. 45

13. Convert 0.28 to a fraction.

    a. 7/25
    b. 3.25
    c. 8/25
    d. 5/28

14. Convert 0.45 to a fraction

   a. 7/20
   b. 7/45
   c. 9/20
   d. 3/20

15. Convert 1/5 to percent.

   a. 10%
   b. 5%
   c. 20%
   d. 25%

16. Convert 0.55 to percent

   a. 45%
   b. 15%
   c. 75%
   d. 55%

17. A man buys an item for $420 and has a balance of $3000.00. How much did he have before?

   a. $2,580
   b. $3,420
   c. $2,420
   d. $342

18. Divide 9.60 by 3.2

   a. 2.50
   b. 3
   c. 2.3
   d. 6.4

Word Problems

19. Two trains leave a station at the same time. One has an average speed of 72 km/hr. and the other 52 km/hr. How far apart are they in 20 minutes?

   a. 6.67 km.
   b. 17.33 km.
   c. 24.3 km.
   d. 41.33 km.

20. The average weight of 13 students in a class of 15 (two were absent that day) is 42 kg. When the remaining two are weighed, the average became 42.7 kg. If one of the remaining students weighs 48, how much does the other weigh?

   a. 44.7 kg.
   b. 45.6 kg.
   c. 46.5 kg.
   d. 47.4 kg.

21. The total expense of building a fence around a square-shaped field is $2000 at a rate of $5 per meter. What is the length of one side?

   a. 40 meters
   b. 80 meters
   c. 100 meters
   d. 320 meters

22. Two trains started at the same time from points 200 km. apart. The first train travels at 40 km/hr and the second train travels at 65 km/hr. How many minutes will it take them to cross?

   a. 92 minutes
   b. 106 minutes
   c. 114 minutes
   d. 118 minutes

23. A person earns $25,000 and pays $9,000 income tax per year. The Government increased income tax by 0.5% per month and his monthly earning was increased $11,000. How much more income tax will he pay per month?

   a. $1260
   b. $1050
   c. $750
   d. $510

24. A company gives a 12% discount to customers on the retail price, and on total purchases over $10,000, they give an additional 3% discount. A customer's total came to $13,500 (discounted price). How much did he save?

   a. $2315
   b. $1850
   c. $2025
   d. $2225

25. Brian jogged 7 times around a circular track 75 meters in diameter. How much linear distance did he cover?

    a. 1250 meters
    b. 1450 meters
    c. 1650 meters
    d. 1725 meters

Answer Key

Basic Math

1. C
389 + 454 = 843

2. C
9,177 + 7,204 = 16,381

3. A
643 - 587 = 56

4. C
3,406 - 2,767 = 639

5. B
149 × 7 = 1043

6. A
467 × 41 = 19,147

7. A
491 ÷ 9 = 54 r5

Decimals, Percent and Fractions

8. C
Total no. of balls = 10, no. of yellow balls = 2, answer = 2/10 X 100 = 20%

9. B
10% of 300 = 30 and 50% of 20 = 10 so 30 + 1- = 40.

10. C
75% = 75/100 = ¾

11. B
25% of 40 = 10 and 10 x 3 = 30

12. A
10% of 30 = 3 and 75% of 200 = 150, 3 X 150 = 450

13. A
0.28 = 28/100 = 7/25

14. C
0.45 = 45/100 = 9/20

15. C
1/5 X 100 = 20%

16. D
0.55 X 100 = 55%

17. B
(Amount Spent) $420 + $3000 (Balance) = $3420

18. B
9.60/3.2 = 3

Word Problems

19. A
Distance traveled by 1st train in 20 minutes = (72 km/hr × 20 minutes) /60 minutes = 24 km. Distance traveled by 2nd train in 20 minutes = (52 km/hr × 20 minutes)/60 minutes = 17.33 km. Difference in distance = 24 - 17.33 = 6.67 km

20. C
Total weight of 13 students with average 42 will be = 42 * 13 = 546 kg.

The total weight of the remaining 2 will be found by subtracting the total weight of 13 students from the total weight of 15 students: 640.5 - 546 = 94.5 kg.

94.5 = the total weight of two students. One of these students weigh 48 kg, so;

The weight of the other will be = 94.5 – 48 = 46.5 kg

21. C
Total expense is $2000 and we are informed that $5 is spent per meter. Combining these two information, we know that the total length of the fence is 2000/5 = 400 meters.

The fence is built around a square-shaped field. If one side of the square is "a," the perimeter of the square is "4a." Here, the perimeter is equal to 400 meters. So,

400 = 4a

100 = a → this means that one side of the square is equal to 100 meters

22. C
Let the time to cross be x hours. The equation will be
40x + 65x = 200
X = 1.9047 hours
X = 1.9047 X 60 = 114.28 minutes

23. D
The income tax per year is $9,000. So, the income tax per month is 9,000/12 = $750.

This person earns $25,000 per month and pays $750 income tax. We need to find the rate of the income tax:

Tax rate: 750 * 100/25,000 = 3%

Government increased this rate by 0.5% so it became 3.5%.

The income of the person per month is increased $11,000 so it became: $25,000 + $11,000 = $36,000.

The new monthly income tax is: 36,000•3.5/100 = $1260.

Amount of increase in tax per month is: $1260 - $750 = $510.

24. A
To calculate the balance before the 3% was taken solve the equation: 13500 = 0.97x, x = 13917.53 Then use this number to solve what the total was before the 12% discount, with the equation: 13917.53 = 0.88x, x = 15,815.37. Then subtract 13500 from this to get a savings of $2315

25. C

In one round-trip, he covers the distance equal to the circumference of the circular path.

Circumference/Diameter = π = 3.14159
75/X = 3.14159
75 X 3.14159 = X

Circumference of the path = X = 235.65 meters.

Distance covered 7 times around = 235.65 × 7 = 1650 meters.

Basic Math Video Tutorials

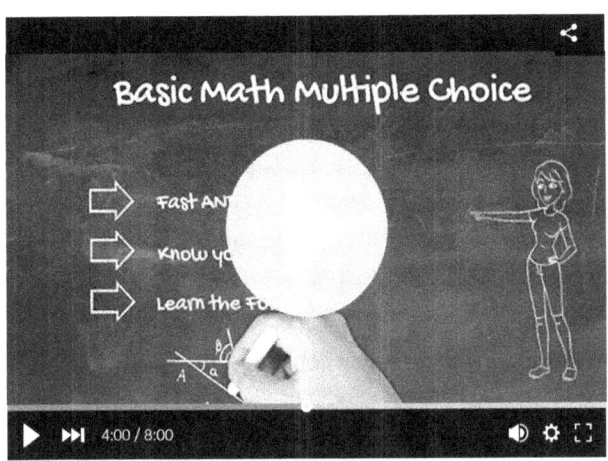

https://test-preparation.ca/basic-math-video-tutorials/

Fraction Tips, Tricks and Shortcuts

When you are writing an exam, time is precious, so anything you can do to answer questions faster is a real advantage.

Here are some ideas, shortcuts, tips and tricks that can speed up answering fraction problems.

Remember that a fraction is just a number which names a portion of something. For instance, instead of having a whole pie, a fraction says you have a part of a pie--such as a half of one or a fourth of one.

Two numbers make up a fraction. The number on top is the numerator. The number on the bottom is the denominator.

To remember which is which, just remember that "denominator" and "down" both start with a "d." And the "downstairs" number is the denominator. So for instance, in ½, the numerator is 1, and the denominator (or "downstairs") number is 2.

Adding Fractions

It's easy to add two fractions if they have the same denominator. Just add the digits on top and leave the bottom one the same: 1/10 + 6/10 = 7/10.

It's the same with subtracting fractions with the same denominator: 7/10 - 6/10 = 1/10.

Adding and subtracting fractions with different denominators is a little more complicated.

First, you have to arrange the fractions so they have the same denominators.

The easiest way to do this is to multiply the denominators: For 2/5 + 1/2 multiply 5 by 2. Now you have a denominator of 10.

But now you have to change the top numbers too. Since you multiplied the 5 in 2/5 by 2, you also multiply the 2 by 2, to get 4. So the first fraction is now 4/10.

In the second fraction, you multiplied the denominator by 5, you have to multiply the numerator by 5 also, to get 5/10.

Now you have 4/10 + 5/10 and you can add 5 and 4 to get 9/10.

Simplest Form

To reduce a fraction to its simplest form, you have to arrange the numerator and denominator so the only common factor is 1.

Think of it this way:

Let's take an example: The fraction 2/10.

This is not reduced to its simplest terms because there is a number that will divide evenly into both: 2. We want to make it so that the only number that will divide evenly into both is 1.

Divide the top and bottom by 2 to get the new, reduced fraction - 1/5.

Multiplying Fractions

This is the easiest of all: Just multiply the two top numbers and then multiply the two bottom numbers.

Here is an example,

2/5 X 2/3

First, multiply the numerators: 2 X 2 = 4

then multiply the denominators: 5 X 3 = 15

Your answer is 4/15.

Dividing Fractions

Dividing fractions is easy if you remember a simple trick - first turn the second fraction upside down - then multiply!

Here is an example:

7/8 X 1/2

Turn the second fraction upside down:

7/8 X 2/1

then multiply:

(7 X 2) / (8 X 1) = 14/8

Converting Fractions to Decimals

There are a couple of ways to become good at converting fractions to decimals. One -- the one that will make you the fastest in basic math skills -- is to learn some basic fraction facts. It's a good idea, if you're good at memory, to memorize the following:

1/100 is "one hundredth," expressed as a decimal, it's .01.

1/50 is "two hundredths," expressed as a decimal, it's .02.

1/25 is "one twenty-fifths" or "four hundredths," expressed as a decimal, it's .04.

1/20 is "one twentieth" or ""five hundredths," expressed as a decimal, it's .05.

1/10 is "one tenth," expressed as a decimal, it's .1.

1/8 is "one eighth," or "one hundred twenty-five thousandths," expressed as a decimal, it's .125.

1/5 is "one fifth," or "two tenths," expressed as a decimal, it's .2.

1/4 is "one fourth" or "twenty-five hundredths," expressed as a decimal, it's .25.

1/3 is "one third" or "thirty-three hundredths," expressed as a decimal, it's .33.

1/2 is "one half" or "five tenths," expressed as a decimal, it's .5.

3/4 is "three fourths," or "seventy-five hundredths," expressed as a decimal, it's .75.

Of course, if you're no good at memorization, another good technique for converting a fraction to a decimal is to manipulate it so that the fraction's denominator is 10, 10, 1000, or some other power of 10. Here's an example: We'll start with ¾. What is the first number in the 4 "times table" that you can multiply and get a multiple of 10? Can you multiply 4 by something to get 10? No. Can you multiply it by something to get 100? Yes! 4 X 25 is 100. So let's take that 25 and multiply it by the numerator in our fraction ¾. The numerator is 3, and 3 X 25 is 75. We'll move the decimal in 75 all the way to the left, and we find that ¾ is .75.

We'll do another one: 1/5. Again, we want to find a power of 10 that 5 goes into evenly. Will 5 go into 10? Yes! It goes 2 times. So we'll take that 2 and multiply it by our numerator, 1, and we get 2. We move the decimal in 2 all the way to the left and find that 1/5 is equal to .2.

Converting Fractions to Percent

Working with fractions or percent can be intimidating enough. But converting from one to the other? That's a genuine nightmare for those who are not math wizards. However, it doesn't have to be that way. Here are two ways to make it easier and faster to convert a fraction to a percent.

- First, you might remember that a fraction is nothing more than a division problem: you're dividing the bottom number into the top number. So for instance, if we start with a fraction 1/10, we are making a division problem with the 10 on the outside the bracket and the 1 on the inside. As you remember from your lessons on dividing by decimals, since 10 won't go into 1, you add a decimal and make it 10 into 1.0. 10 into 10 goes 1 time, and since it's behind the decimal, it's .1. And how do we say .1? We say "one tenth," which is exactly what we started with: 1/10. So we have a number we can work with now: .1. When we're dealing with percents, though, we're dealing strictly with hundredths (not tenths). You remember from studying decimals that adding a zero to the right, on the right side of the decimal does not change the value. Therefore, we can change .1 into .10 and have the same number--except now it's expressed as hundredths. We have 10 hundredths. That's ten out of 100--which is just another way of saying ten percent (ten per hundred or ten out of

100). In other words .1 = .10 = 10 percent. Remember, if you're changing from a decimal to a percent, get rid of the decimal on the left and replace it with a percent mark on the right: 10%. Let's review those steps again: Divide 10 into 1. Since 10 doesn't go into 1, turn 1 into 1.0. Now divide 10 into 1.0. Since 10 goes into 10 1 time, put it there and add your decimal to make it .1. Since a percent is always "hundredths," let's change .1 into .10. Then remove the decimal on the left and replace with a percent sign on the right. The answer is 10%.

☐ If you're doing these conversions on a multiple-choice test, here's an idea that might be even easier and faster. Let's say you have a fraction of 1/8 and you're asked what the percent is. Since we know that "percent" means hundredths, ask yourself what number we can multiply 8 by to get 100. Since there is no number, ask what number gets us close to 100. That number is 12: 8 X 12 = 96. So it gets us a little less than 100. Now, whatever you do to the denominator, you have to do to the numerator. Let's multiply 1 X 12 and we get 12. However, since 96 is a little less than 100, we know that our answer will be a percent a little MORE than 12%. So if your possible answers on the multiple-choice test are these:

a) 8.5%   b) 19%   c) 12.5%   d) 25%

then we know the answer is c) 12.5%, because it's a little MORE than the 12 we got in our math problem above.

Another way to look at this, using multiple choice strategy is you know the answer will be "about" 12. Looking at the other choices, they are all either too large or too small and can be eliminated right away.

This was an easy example to demonstrate, so don't be fooled! You probably won't get such an easy question on your exam, but the principle holds just the same. By estimating your answer quickly, you can eliminate choices immediately and save precious exam time.

Decimal Tips, Tricks and Shortcuts

Converting decimals to fractions is easy if you say it the right way! If you say "point one" or "point 25", you'll have trouble.

But if you say, "one tenth" and "twenty-five hundredths," then you have already solved it! That's because, if you know your fractions, you know that "one tenth" looks like this: 1/10. And "twenty-five hundredths" looks like this: 25/100.

Even if you have digits before the decimal, such as 3.4, learning how to say the word will help you with the conversion into a fraction. It's not "three point four," it's "three and four tenths." Knowing this, you know that the fraction which looks like "three and four tenths" is 3 4/10.

The conversion is not complete until you reduce the fraction to its lowest terms: It's not 25/100, but 1/4.

Converting Decimals to Percent

Changing a decimal to a percent is easy if you remember one thing: multiply by 100.

For example, if you start with .45, simply multiply it by 100 for 45. Then add the % sign to the end - 45%.

Think of it this way: take out the decimal point, add a percent sign on the opposite side. In other words, the decimal on the left is replaced by the % on the right.

It doesn't work quite that easily if the decimal is in the middle of the number. For example, 3.7. Here, take out the decimal in the middle and replace it with a 0 % at the end. So 3.7 converted to decimal is 370%.

Percent Tips, Tricks and Shortcuts

Percent problems are not nearly as scary as they appear, if you remember this neat trick:

Draw a cross as in:

Portion	Percent
Whole	100

In the upper left, write PORTION. In the bottom left, write WHOLE. In the top right, write PERCENT and in the bottom right, write 100. Whatever your problem is, you will leave blank the unknown, and fill in the other four parts. For example, let's suppose your problem is: Find 10% of 50. Since we know the 10% part, we put 10 in the percent corner. Since the whole number in our problem is 50, we put that in the corner marked whole. You always put 100 underneath the percent, so we leave it as is, which leaves only the top left corner blank. This is where we'll put our answer. Now simply multiply the two corner numbers that are NOT 100. Here, it's 10 X 50. That gives us 500. Now divide this by the remaining corner, or 100, to get a final answer of 5. 5 is the number that goes in the upper-left corner, and is your final solution.

Another hint to remember: Percents are the same thing as hundredths in decimals. So .45 is the same as 45 hundredths or 45 percent.

Converting Percents to Decimals

Percents are a type of decimal, so it should be no surprise that converting between the two is actually fairly simple. Here are a few tricks and shortcuts to keep in mind:

- Remember that percent literally means "per 100" or "for every 100." So when you speak of 30% you're saying 30 for every 100 or the fraction 30/100. In basic math, you learned that fractions that have 10 or 100 as the denominator can easily be turned to a decimal. 30/100 is thirty hundredths, or expressed as a decimal, .30.
- Another way to look at it: To convert a percent to a decimal, simply divide the number by 100. So for instance, if the percent is 47%, divide 47 by 100. The result will be .47. Get rid of the % mark and you're done.
- Remember that the easiest way of dividing by 100 is by moving your decimal two spots to the left.

Converting Percents to Fractions

Converting percents to fractions is easy. After all, a percent is just a type of fraction; it tells you what part of 100 that you're talking about. Here are some simple ideas for making the conversion from a percent to a fraction:

- If the percent is a whole number -- say 34% -- then simply write a fraction with 100 as the denominator (the bottom number). Then put the percentage itself on top. So 34% becomes 34/100.
- Now reduce as you would reduce any percent. Here, by dividing 2 into 34 and 2 into 100, you get 17/50.
- If your percent is not a whole number -- say 3.4% --then convert it to a decimal expressed as hundredths. 3.4 is the same as 3.40 (or 3 and forty hundredths). Now ask yourself how you would express "three and forty hundredths" as a fraction. It would, of course, be 3 40/100. Reduce this and it becomes 3 2/5.

How to Answer Basic Math Multiple Choice

Math is the one section where you need to make sure that you understand the processes before you ever tackle it. That's because the time allowed on the math portion is typically so short that there's not much room for error. You have to be fast and accurate. It's imperative that before the test day arrives, you've learned all of the main formulas that will be used, and then to create your own problems (and solve them).

On the actual test day, use the "Plug-Check-Check" strategy. Here's how it goes.

Read the problem, but not the answers. You'll want to work the problem first and come up with your own answers. If you did the work right, you should find your answer among the choices.

If you need help with the problem, plug actual numbers into the variables given. You'll find it easier to work with numbers than it is to work with letters. For instance, if the question asks, "If Y - 4 is 2 more than Z, then Y + 5 is how much more than Z?" try selecting a value for Y. Let's take 6. Your question now becomes, "If 6 - 4 is 2 more than Z, then 6 plus 5 is how much more than Z?" Now your answer should be easier to work with.

Check the answer choices to see if your answer matches one of those. If so, select it.

If no answer matches the one you got, re-check your math, but this time, use a different method. In math, it's common for there to be more than one way to solve a problem. As a simple example, if you multiplied 12 X 13 and did not get an answer that matches one of the answer choices, you might try adding 13 together 12 different times and see if you get a good answer.

Math Multiple Choice Strategy

The time allowed on the math portion of a standardized test is typically so short that there's no room for error. You have to be fast and accurate.

Math strategy is very helpful, but nothing beats knowing your stuff! Make sure that you have learned all the important formulas that will be used.

If you don't know the formulas, strategy won't help you.

How to Answer Basic Math Questions - the Basics

First, read the problem, but not the answers.

Work through the problem first and come up with your own answers. Hopefully, you should find your answer among the choices.

If no answer matches the one you got, re-check your math, but this time, use a different method. In math, there are different ways to solve a problem.

Math Multiple Choice Strategy

The two strategies for working with basic math multiple choice are Estimation and Elimination.

Estimation is just as it sounds - try to estimate an approximate answer first. Then look at the choices.

Elimination is probably the most powerful strategy for answering multiple choice.

Eliminate obviously incorrect answers and narrowing the possible choices.

Here are a few basic math examples of how this works.

Solve 2/3 + 5/12

    a. 9/17

    b. 3/11

    c. 7/12

    d. 1 1/12

First estimate the answer. 2/3 is more than half and 5/12 is about half, so the answer is going to be very close to 1.

Next, Eliminate. Choice A is about 1/2 and can be eliminated, choice B is very small, less than 1/2 and can be eliminated. Choice C is close to 1/2 and can be eliminated. Leaving only choice D, which is just over 1.

Work through the solution, find a common denominator and add. The correct answer is 1 1/12, so Choice D is correct.

Let's look at another example:

Solve 4/5 – 2/3

    a. 2/2

    b. 2/13

    c. 1

    d. 2/15

First, quickly estimate the answer. 4/5 is very close to 1, and 2/3 more than half, so the answer is going to be less than 1/2.

Choice A can be eliminated right away, because it is 1. Choice C can be eliminated for the same reason.

Next, look at the denominators. Since 5 and 3 don't go into 13, choice B can be eliminated as well.

That leaves choice D. Checking the answer, the common denominator will be 15. So the answer is 2/15 and choice D is correct.

Fractions shortcuts - Cancelling out

This is a powerful shortcut that saves you time and simplifies the problem into more manageable numbers!

If the numerator of one fractions has a common multiple with the denominator of the other fraction, you can cancel out.

Solve 2/15 ÷ 4/5

    a. 6/65

    b. 6/75

    c. 5/12

    d. 1/6

To divide fractions, multiply the first fraction with the inverse of the second.

So that gives 2/15 x 5/4. The numerator of the first fraction, 2, shares a multiple with the denominator of the second fraction, 4, which is 2. These cancel out, which gives,

1/15 X 5/2

We can cancel out again, since 15 and 5 are multiples, which gives,

1/3 x 1/2 = 1/6

Cancelling out solved the questions very quickly, but we can still use multiple choice strategies to answer.

Choice B can be eliminated because 75 is too large a denominator. Choice C can be eliminated because 5 and 15 don't go into 12.

Choice D is correct.

Decimal Multiple Choice strategy and Shortcuts

Multiplying decimals gives a very quick way to estimate and eliminate choices. Anytime that you multiply decimals, it is going to give a answer with the same number of decimal places as the combined operands.

So for example,

2.38 X 1.2 will produce a number with three places of decimal, which is 2.856.
Here are a few examples with step-by-step explanation:

Solve 2.06 x 1.2

    a. 24.82

    b. 2.482

    c. 24.72

    d. 2.472

This is a simple question, but even before you start calculating, you can eliminate several choices. When multiplying decimals, there will always be as many numbers behind the decimal place in the answer as the sum of the ones in the initial problem, so Choices A and C can be eliminated.

The correct answer is D: 2.06 x 1.2 = 2.472

Solve 20.0 ÷ 2.5

    a. 12.05

    b. 9.25

    c. 8.3

    d. 8

First estimate the answer to be around 10, and eliminate Choice A. And since it'd also be an even number, you can eliminate Choice B and C., leaving only choice D.

The correct Answer is D: 20.0 ÷ 2.5 = 8

How to Solve Word Problems

Do you know what the biggest tip for solving word problems is?

Practice regularly and systematically.

Sounds simple and easy right? Yes it is, and yes it really does work.

Word problems are a way of thinking and require you to translate a real-world problem into mathematical terms.

Some math teachers say that learning how to think mathematically is the main reason for teaching word problems.

So what does that mean?

Studying word problems and math in general requires a logical and mathematical frame of mind. The only way you can get this is by practicing regularly, which means every day.

It is critical that you practice word problems every day for the 5 days before the exam as the absolute minimum.

If you practice and miss a day, you have lost the mathematical frame of mind and the benefit of your previous practice is gone. You must start all over again.

Everything is important.

All the information given in the problem has some purpose. There is no unnecessary information! Word problems are typically around 50 words in 2 or 3 sentences.

Often, the relationships are complicated. To explain everything, every word counts.

Make sure that you use every piece of information.

Here are 9 simple steps to solve word problems.

Step 1 – Read through the problem at least three times. The first reading should be a quick scan, and the next two readings should be done slowly to find answers to these important questions:

What does the problem ask? (Usually located towards the end of the problem)

What does the problem imply? (This is usually a point you were asked to remember).

Mark all information, and underline all important words or phrases.

Step 2 – Try to make a pictorial representation of the problem such as a circle and an arrow to show travel. This makes the problem a bit more real and sensible to you.

A favorite word problem is something like, 1 train leaves Station A traveling at 100 km/hr and another train leaves Station B traveling at 60 km/hr. ...

Draw a line, the two stations, and the two trains at either end. This will help clarify the situation in your mind.

Step 3 – Use the information you have to make a table with a blank portion to show information you do not know.

Step 4 – Assign a single letter to represent each unknown data in your table. You can write down the unknown that each letter represents so that you do not make the error of assigning answers to the wrong unknown, because a word problem may have multiple unknowns and you will need to create equations for each unknown.

Step 5 – Translate the English terms in the word problem into a mathematical algebraic equation. Remember that the main problem with word problems is that they are not expressed in regular math equations. You ability to identify correctly the variables and translate the word problem into an equation determines your ability to solve the problem.

Step 6 – Check the equation to see if it looks like regular equations that you have seen before, and whether it looks sensible. Does the equation appear to represent the information in the question? Take note that you may need to rewrite some formulas needed to solve the word problem equation. For example, word distance problems may need rewriting the distance formula, which is Distance = Time x Rate. If the word problem requires that you solve for time you will need to use Distance/Rate and Distance/Time to solve for Rate. If you understand the distance word problem you should be able to identify the variable you need to solve for.

Step 7 – Use algebra rules to solve the derived equation. Take note that the laws of equation demands that what is done on this side of the equation has to also be done on the other side. You have to solve the equation so that the unknown ends up alone on one side. Where there are multiple unknowns you will need to use elimination or substitution methods to resolve all the equations.

Step 8 – Check your final answers to see if they make sense with the information given in the problem. For example if the word problem involves a discount, the final price should be less or if a product was taxed then the final answer has to cost more.

Step 9 – Cross check your answers by placing the answer or answers in the first equation to replace the unknown or unknowns. If your answer is correct then both side of the equation must equate or equal. If your answer is not correct then you may have derived a wrong equation or solved the equation wrongly. Repeat the necessary steps to correct.

Types of Word Problems

Word problems can be classified into 12 types. Below are examples of each type with a complete solution. Some types of word problems can be solved quickly using multiple choice strategies and some cannot. Always look for ways to estimate the answer and then eliminate choices.

1. Age

A girl is 10 years older than her brother. By next year, she will be twice the age of her brother. What are their ages now?

    a. 25, 15
    b. 19, 9
    c. 21, 11
    d. 29, 19

Solution: B

We will assume that the girl's age is "a" and her brother's is "b." This means that based on the information in the first sentence,
$a = 10 + b$

Next year, she will be twice her brother's age, which gives
$a + 1 = 2(b + 1)$

We need to solve for one unknown factor and then use the answer to solve for the other. To do this we substitute the value of "a" from the first equation into the second equation. This gives

$10 + b + 1 = 2b + 2$
$11 + b = 2b + 2$
$11 - 2 = 2b - b$
$b = 9$

9 = b this means that her brother is 9 years old. Solving for the girl's age in the first equation gives a = 10 + 9. a = 19 the girl is aged 19. So, the girl is aged 19 and the boy is 9

2. Distance or speed

Two boats travel down a river towards the same destination, starting at the same time. One boat is traveling at 52 km/hr, and the other boat at 43 km/hr. How far apart will they be after 40 minutes?

   a. 46.67 km
   b. 19.23 km
   c. 6.04 km
   d. 14.39 km

Solution: C

After 40 minutes, the first boat will have traveled = 52 km/hr x 40 minutes/60 minutes = 34.7 km
After 40 minutes, the second boat will have traveled = 43 km/hr x 40/60 minutes = 28.66 km
Difference between the two boats will be 34.7 km – 28.66 km = 6.04 km.

Multiple Choice Strategy

First estimate the answer. The first boat is travelling 9 km. faster than the second, for 40 minutes, which is 2/3 of an hour. 2/3 of 9 = 6, as a rough guess of the distance apart.

Choices A, B and D can be eliminated right away.

3. Ratio

The instructions in a cookbook states that 700 grams of flour must be mixed in 100 ml of water, and 0.90 grams of salt added. A cook however has just 325 grams of flour. What is the quantity of water and salt that he should use?

    a. 0.41 grams and 46.4 ml
    b. 0.45 grams and 49.3 ml
    c. 0.39 grams and 39.8 ml
    d. 0.25 grams and 40.1 ml

Solution: A

The Cookbook states 700 grams of flour, but the cook only has 325. The first step is to determine the percentage of flour he has 325/700 x 100 = 46.4%
That means that 46.4% of all other items must also be used.
46.4% of 100 = 46.4 ml of water
46.4% of 0.90 = 0.41 grams of salt.

Multiple Choice Strategy

The recipe calls for 700 grams of flour but the cook only has 325, which is just less than half, the amount of water and salt are going to be about half.

Choices C and D can be eliminated right away. Choice B is very close so be careful. Looking closely at Choice B, it is exactly half, and since 325 is slightly less than half of 700, it can't be correct.

Choice A is correct.

4. Percent

An agent received $6,685 as his commission for selling a property. If his commission was 13% of the selling price, how much was the property?

 a. $68,825
 b. $121,850
 c. $49,025
 d. $51,423

Solution: D

Let's assume that the property price is x
That means from the information given, 13% of x = 6,685
Solve for x,
x = 6685 x 100/13 = $51,423

Multiple Choice Strategy

The commission, 13%, is just over 10%, which is easier to work with. Round up $6685 to $6700, and multiple by 10 for an approximate answer. 10 X 6700 = $67,000. You can do this in your head. Choice B is much too big and can be eliminated. Choice C is too small and can be eliminated. Choices A and D are left and good possibilities.

Do the calculations to make the final choice.

5. Sales & Profit

A store owner buys merchandise for $21,045. He transports them for $3,905 and pays his staff $1,450 to stock the merchandise on his shelves. If he does not incur further costs, how much does he need to sell the items to make $5,000 profit?

 a. $32,500
 b. $29,350
 c. $32,400
 d. $31,400

Solution: D

Total cost of the items is $21,045 + $3,905 + $1,450 = $26,400
Total cost is now $26,400 + $5000 profit = $31,400

Multiple Choice Strategy

Round off and add the numbers up in your head quickly.
21,000 + 4,000 + 1500 = 26500. Add in 5000 profit for a total of 31500.

Choice B is too small and can be eliminated. Choice C and A are too large and can be eliminated.

6. Tax/Income

A woman earns $42,000 per month and pays 5% tax on her monthly income. If the Government increases her monthly taxes by $1,500, what is her income after tax?

- a. $38,400
- b. $36,050
- c. $40,500
- d. $39, 500

Solution: A

Initial tax on income was 5/100 x 42,000 = $2,100
$1,500 was added to the tax to give $2,100 + 1,500 = $3,600
Income after tax left is $42,000 - $3,600 = $38,400

7. Interest

A man invests $3000 in a 2-year term deposit that pays 3% interest per year. How much will he have at the end of the 2-year term?

- a. $5,200
- b. $3,020
- c. $3,182.7
- d. $3,000

Solution: C

This is a compound interest problem. The funds are invested for 2 years and interest is paid yearly, so in the second year, he will earn interest on the interest paid in the first year.

3% interest in the first year = 3/100 x 3,000 = $90
At end of first year, total amount = 3,000 + 90 = $3,090
Second year = 3/100 x 3,090 = 92.7.
At end of second year, total amount = $3090 + $92.7 = $3,182.7

8. Averaging

The average weight of 10 books is 54 grams. 2 more books were added and the average weight became 55.4. If one of the 2 new books added weighed 62.8 g, what is the weight of the other?

    a. 44.7 g
    b. 67.4 g
    c. 62 g
    d. 52 g

Solution: C
Total weight of 10 books with average 54 grams will be = 10 × 54 = 540 g
Total weight of 12 books with average 55.4 will be = 55.4 × 12 = 664.8 g
So total weight of the remaining 2 will be= 664.8 – 540 = 124.8 g
If one weighs 62.8, the weight of the other will be= 124.8 g – 62.8 g = 62 g

Multiple Choice Strategy

Averaging problems can be estimated by looking at which direction the average goes. If additional items are added and the average goes up, the new items much be greater than the average. If the average goes down after new items are added, the new items must be less than the average.
Here, the average is 54 grams and 2 books are added which

increases the average to 55.4, so the new books must weight more than 54 grams.

Choices A and D can be eliminated right away.

9. Probability

A bag contains 15 marbles of various colors. If 3 marbles are white, 5 are red and the rest are black, what is the probability of randomly picking out a black marble from the bag?

    a. 7/15
    b. 3/15
    c. 1/5
    d. 4/15

Solution: A

Total marbles = 15
Number of black marbles = 15 − (3 + 5) = 7
Probability of picking out a black marble = 7/15

10. Two Variables

A company paid a total of $2850 to book for 6 single rooms and 4 double rooms in a hotel for one night. Another company paid $3185 to book for 13 single rooms for one night in the same hotel. What is the cost for single and double rooms in that hotel?

    a. single= $250 and double = $345
    b. single= $254 and double = $350
    c. single = $245 and double = $305
    d. single = $245 and double = $345

Solution: D

We can determine the price of single rooms from the information given of the second company. 13 single rooms = 3185.
One single room = 3185 / 13 = 245

The first company paid for 6 single rooms at $245. 245 x 6 = $1470
Total amount paid for 4 double rooms by first company = $2850 - $1470 = $1380
Cost per double room = 1380 / 4 = $345

11. Geometry

The length of a rectangle is 5 in. more than its width. The perimeter of the rectangle is 26 in. What is the width and length of the rectangle?

    a. width = 6 inches, Length = 9 inches
    b. width = 4 inches, Length = 9 inches
    c. width =4 inches, Length = 5 inches
    d. width = 6 inches, Length = 11 inches

Solution: B

Formula for perimeter of a rectangle is 2(L + W)
p=26, so 2(L+W) = p
The length is 5 inches more than the width, so
2(w+5) + 2w = 26
2w + 10 + 2w = 26
2w + 2w = 26 - 10
4w = 16

W = 16/4 = 4 inches

L is 5 inches more than w, so L = 5 + 4 = 9 inches.

12. Totals and fractions

A basket contains 125 oranges, mangos and apples. If 3/5 of the fruits in the basket are mangos and only 2/5 of the mangos are ripe, how many ripe mangos are there in the basket?

    a. 30
    b. 68
    c. 55
    d. 47

Solution: A
Number of mangos in the basket is 3/5 x 125 = 75
Number of ripe mangos = 2/5 x 75 = 30
5
Number of ripe mangos = 2/5 x 75 = 30

Mechanical Comprehension

THIS SECTION CONTAINS A MECHANICAL COMPREHENSION SELF-ASSESSMENT. The self-assessment contains general questions similar to the questions likely to be on the exam, but are not intended to be identical to the exam questions.

Below is a Mechanical Comprehension Self-assessment. The purpose of the self-assessment is:

- Identify your strengths and weaknesses.
- Develop your personalized study plan (above)
- Get accustomed to the format
- Extra practice – the self-assessments are almost a full 3rd practice test!

Since this is a self-assessment, and depending on how confident you are with Mechanical Comprehension, timing yourself is optional. Most firefighter tests have about 25 questions, so allow yourself about one minute per question.

The questions below are not the same as you will find on the Gledhill Shaw exam - that would be too easy! And nobody knows what the questions will be and they change all the time. Below are general mechanical comprehension questions that cover the same areas as the Gledhill Shaw exam. So, while the format and exact wording of the questions may differ slightly, and change from year to year, if you can answer the questions below, you will have no problem with the mechanical comprehension section of the Gledhill Shaw exam.

The self-assessment is designed to give you a baseline score in the different areas covered. Here is a brief outline of how your score on the self-assessment relates to your understanding of the material.

75% - 100%	Excellent – you have mastered the content
50 – 75%	Good. You have a working knowledge. Even though you can just pass this section, you may want to review the tutorials and do some extra practice to see if you can improve your mark.
25% - 50%	Below Average. You do not understand the content. Review the tutorials, and retake this quiz again in a few days, before proceeding to the rest of the practice test questions.
Less than 25%	Poor. You have a very limited understanding. Please review the Tutorials, and retake this quiz again in a few days, before proceeding to the rest of the practice test questions.

Mechanical Comprehension
Self-Assessment

1. Ⓐ Ⓑ Ⓒ Ⓓ
2. Ⓐ Ⓑ Ⓒ Ⓓ
3. Ⓐ Ⓑ Ⓒ Ⓓ
4. Ⓐ Ⓑ Ⓒ Ⓓ
5. Ⓐ Ⓑ Ⓒ Ⓓ
6. Ⓐ Ⓑ Ⓒ Ⓓ
7. Ⓐ Ⓑ Ⓒ Ⓓ
8. Ⓐ Ⓑ Ⓒ Ⓓ
9. Ⓐ Ⓑ Ⓒ Ⓓ
10. Ⓐ Ⓑ Ⓒ Ⓓ

Mechanical Comprehension Self-Assessment

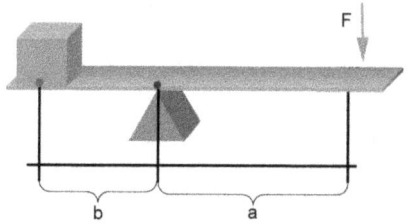

1. Consider the illustration above and the corresponding data:

Weight = W = 200 pounds
Distance from fulcrum to Weight = b = 10 feet
Distance from fulcrum to point where force is applied = a = 20 feet
How much force (F) must be applied to lift the weight?

    a. 80
    b. 100
    c. 150
    d. 200

2. Why does a vehicle overheat more on hot days than on cold days?

    a. The engine works harder and generates more heat.
    b. The cooling fluid is hotter.
    c. The air moving through the radiator isn't sufficient to cool the fluid.
    d. None of the above

3. You are asked to determine the gear ratio of a vehicle. You open the differential and observe the ring gear the and pinion gear. The ring gear has 40 teeth and the pinion gear has 8, What is the gear ratio of the vehicle?

    a. 4:1
    b. 5:1
    c. 8:2
    d. 8:0

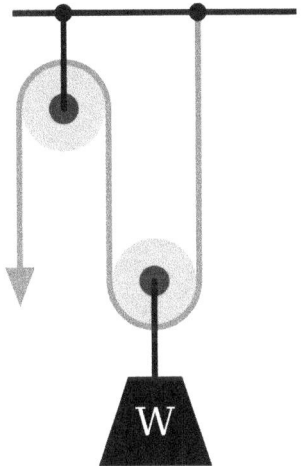

4. Consider the pulley arrangement above. If the weight, W, is 50 pounds, how much force is required to lift it?

    a. 10 pounds
    b. 20 pounds
    c. 25 pounds
    d. 50 pounds

5. Consider a gear train with 3 gears, from left to right, A with 20 teeth, gear B with 60 teeth, and gear C with 10 teeth. Gear A turns clockwise at 60 rpm. What direction and speed in rpm does Gear C turn?

    a. 120 rpm, clockwise

    b. 100 rpm clockwise

    c. 120 rpm counter clockwise

    d. 140 rpm counter clockwise

6. If a 100-pound object is sitting on a 10-square-inch plate, what is the PSI?

    a. 5

    b. 10

    c. 15

    d. 20

7. Consider the gauge above. What is the temperature?

    a. 26° C

    b. 23° C

    c. 22° C

    d. 25° C

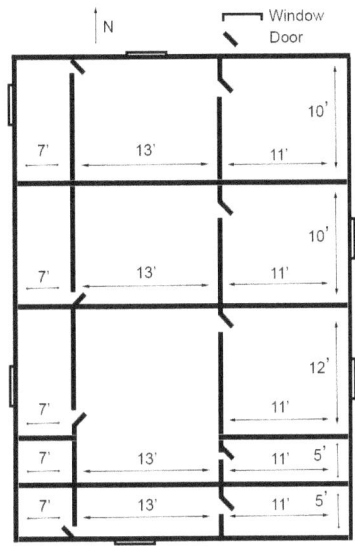

8. What is the length of this house from north to south?

   a. 35 ft
   b. 28 ft
   c. 31 ft.
   d. 36 ft.

9. What is the width of this house from east to west?

   a. 35 ft.
   b. 31 ft.
   c. 28 ft.
   d. 33 ft.

10. Which of the following floor plans corresponds to the house below?

a.

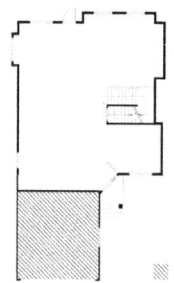

b.

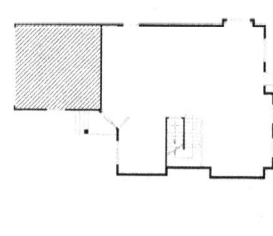

c.

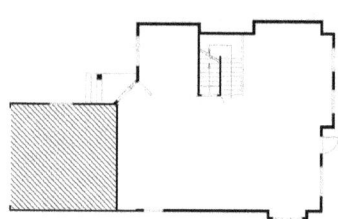

d.

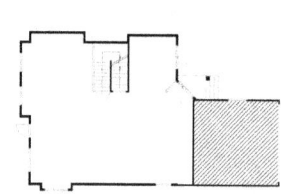

Answer Key

1. B
To solve for F, Weight X b (distance from fulcrum to weight) = Force X a (distance from fulcrum to point where force is applied)
200 X 10 = F X 20
2000/20 = F
F = 100

2. C
Vehicles will tend to overheat more on hot days than on cold days because the air travelling through and around the radiator isn't cold enough to cool the fluid.

3. B
Opening the differential, the ring gear is the larger gear and the pinion the smaller. The gear differential is calculated by dividing the number of teeth on the pinion, into the number of teeth on the ring gear. 40/8 = 5, or 5:1.

4. C
Since the weight is only attached to one pulley, the force required will be 50/2 = 25 pounds.

5. A
First calculate the speed of gear B. The gear ratio is 60:20 or 3:1. If gear A is turning at 60 rpm, then gear B will turn at 30/3 = 20 rpm.

Next calculate B and C. Gear C is smaller, so it will turn faster. The gear ratio is 60:10 or 6:1, and since gear B turns at 20 rpm, gear C will turn at 20 X 6 = 120 rpm.

Next calculate the direction. Gear A is turning clockwise, so Gear B is turning counter clockwise, so Gear C must be turning clockwise.

6. B
Calculate the PSI by taking the weight divided by the size of the object the weight is bearing on. 100/10 = 10 PSI.

7. A

The temperature gauge is showing $26°$

8. A

The length of the house from north to south is 42 ft.

9. B

The width of the house from east to west is 31 ft.

10. A

Floor plan A corresponds to the pictured house.

Mechanical Comprehension Tutorials

Overview of Simple Machines

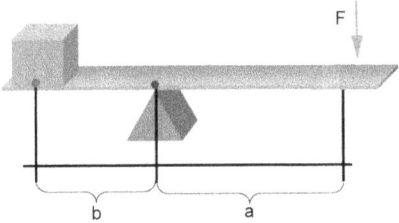

1. Lever

The lever is a movable bar that pivots on a fulcrum attached to a fixed point. The lever operates by applying forces at different distances from the fulcrum, or pivot.

Assuming the lever does not dissipate or store energy, the power into the lever must equal the power out of the lever. As the lever rotates around the fulcrum, points farther from this pivot move faster than points closer to the pivot. Therefore a force applied to a point farther from the pivot must be less than the force located at a point closer in, because power is the product of force and velocity.

This is the law of the lever, which was proven by Archimedes using geometric reasoning. It shows that if the distance a from the fulcrum to where the input force is applied (point A) is greater than the distance b from fulcrum to where the output force is applied (point B), then the lever amplifies the input force. On the other hand, if the distance a from the fulcrum to the input force is less than the distance b from the fulcrum to the output force, then the lever reduces the input force.

Here is a sample question:

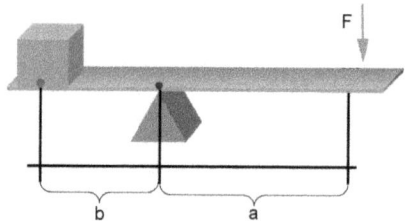

Consider the illustration above and the corresponding data:

Weight = W = 100 pounds
Distance from fulcrum to Weight = b = 2 feet
Distance from fulcrum to point where force is applied = a = 5 feet
How much force (F) must be applied to lift the weight?

    a. 100

    b. 40

    c. 25

    d. 10

Answer: B
Solution: We know that the lever does not store energy, so the to solve for F, Weight X b (distance from fulcrum to weight) = Force X a (distance from fulcrum to point where force is applied)
100 X 2 = F X 5
200/5 = F
F = 40

2. Pulley

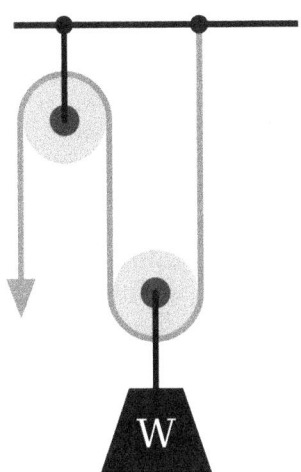

A pulley is a wheel on an axle that is designed to support movement of a cable or belt along its circumference. Pulleys are used in a variety of ways to lift loads, apply forces, and to transmit power.

A pulley is also called a sheave or drum and may have a groove between two flanges around its circumference. The drive element of a pulley system can be a rope, cable, belt, or chain that runs over the pulley inside the groove.

A rope and pulley system, that is a block and tackle, is characterized by a single continuous rope to transmit a tension force around one or more pulleys to lift or move a load—the rope may be a light line or a strong cable.

If the rope and pulley system does not dissipate or store energy, then its mechanical advantage is the number of parts of the rope that act on the load. This can be shown as follows.

Consider the set of pulleys that form the moving block and the parts of the rope that support this block. If there are p of these parts of the rope supporting the load W, then a force balance on the moving block shows that the tension in each of the parts of the rope must be W/p. This means the input force on the rope is T=W/p. Thus, the block and tackle reduces the input force by the factor p.

3. Wedge

A wedge is a triangular shaped round tool, a compound and portable inclined plane, and one of the six classical simple machines. It can be used to separate two objects or portions of an object, lift an object, or hold an object in place. It functions by converting a force applied to its blunt end into forces perpendicular (normal) to its inclined surfaces. The mechanical advantage of a wedge is given by the ratio of the length of its slope to its width. Although a short wedge with a wide angle may do a job faster, it requires more force than a long wedge with a narrow angle.

Gears and Gear Trains

A gear train is formed by mounting gears on a frame so that the teeth of the gears engage. Gear teeth are designed to ensure the pitch circles of engaging gears roll on each other without slipping, this provides a smooth transmission of rotation from one gear to the next.

Here is a sample question:

Consider 3 meshed gears. Gear A has 20 teeth, Gear B has 60 teeth and Gear C has 10 teeth. Gear A revolves clockwise at 60 rpm. How fast does gear C turn and in what direction?

First, figure out the direction because that is easier. Gear A turn clockwise, which will turn gear B counter-clockwise. Now gear C, meshed with gear B will turn clockwise.

To calculate the speed of gear C, first calculate the speed of gear B.

To calculate the speed of gear B, first calculate the gear ration by,
No. of teeth of gear B / No. of teeth of gear A

60/20 = 3 (or gear ratio of 1:3 : Gear B : Gear A)

So gear B will turn 3 times for every complete turn of gear A.

To calculate the speed of gear B, divide, 60/3 = 20 rpm.

This makes sense since gear B is three times the size of gear A (60 teeth to gear A's 20) so it turns much slower.

To calculate the speed of gear C, calculate the gear ration and then divide by the speed of gear B.

Notice that gear C is quite a bit smaller (10 teeth to gear B's 60 teeth), so we expect gear C will turn much faster.

First calculate the gear ratio: 60/10 = 6, or 6:1 : Gear C : Gear B.

Gear B is turning at 20 rpm - multiplying the speed is, 20 rpm X 6 = 120.

Gear C is turning at 120 rpm.

Dealing with People Situation Judgment

The Dealing with People section is a Situational Judgment Test (SJT). This section evaluates your ability to work effectively with others including

- interpersonal skills
- communication skills
- teamwork
- community interaction

The questions below are not the same as you will find on the Gledhill Shaw exam - that would be too easy! And nobody knows what the questions will be and they change all the time. Below are general situation judgment questions that cover the same areas as the Gledhill Shaw exam. So, while the format and exact wording of the questions may differ slightly, and change from year to year, if you can answer the questions below, you will have no problem with the situation judgment section of the Gledhill Shaw exam.

Scenario 1

An editor complains about your work regardless of how much you try. How should you deal with a difficult supervisor?

    a. Ignore his negative comments and stay positive

    b. Listen attentively to the criticism and try to comply.

    c. Refer to the company's policy document for further information.

    d. Blame the supervisor for being ignorant.

Scenario 2

Workload is increasingly becoming a problem in your department. How should you work to improve the situation?

    a. Assign more work to a junior employees as well as divide the work more efficiently.

    b. Request more staff or temporary help from the management.

    c. Ask for higher pay for you and your team.

    d. Do what you can and leave what you can't.

Scenario 3

You have been given an assignment together with a colleague. When you need crucial information, your colleague takes too long time to respond. What should you do?

    a. Discuss with your colleague and see if there is a solution.

    b. Discuss the matter with your immediate supervisor.

    c. Demand that he keeps you posted at all times and respond faster.

    d. Acquire information from other sources on your own.

Scenario 4

The company you work for undergoes various changes. You, and some of the employees, are finding it hard to adjust to rapid and constant changes. How should you act in such a situation?

    a. Rebel against the proposed changes.

    b. Read new company books to improve yourself.

    c. Mobilize other employees to attend training.

    d. Become more actively involved in the changes.

Scenario 5

You face a lot of criticism at work for something you did. This weighs you down and affects your general performance. What should you do?

    a. Find areas to criticize those criticizing you.

    b. Let the matter be addressed by your supervisors.

    c. Resent the critic.

    d. Work on improving the aspect criticized by my colleagues.

Scenario 6

Some of the junior employees in your company are not under your jurisdiction yet their co-operation is important for the success of your business. How should you handle the situation?

    a. Demand for cooperation from them.

    b. Call them to a meeting and stress on the fact that you are a boss and they need to cooperate.

    c. Clearly communicate your ideas and be open to feedback.

    d. Request their supervisors to order them to cooperate with your department.

Scenario 7

The company you are working for has experienced communication hiccups and misunderstandings in the past. How should you prevent similar incidents in the future?

    a. Encourage all employees to use written communication.

    b. Make clarifications where needed and encourage team members to do the same.

    c. Refuse to consider any verbal communication.

    d. Be complacent in communicating with others.

Scenario 8

A workmate is very mean to you. You disregard this but the issue has recently been putting a lot pressure on you. You need to stay positive and motivated. How should you handle this?

    a. Become mean to them as well.

    b. Confront his ill behavior.

    c. Involve supervisors in resolving the conflict.

    d. Keep on motivating yourself to become better.

Scenario 9

Bob is new to the office staff. Your superior, has assigned you to teach Bob the computer system due to your experience. It is a relatively simple system, however, Bob is finding it difficult to understand.

What should you do?

> a. Tell him it should be easy for everyone to understand and he needs to learn it quickly.
>
> b. Allow Anna, who has more experience than you, to conduct the lesson. Return to your other activities for the rest of the day.
>
> c. Tell Bob to do it later. You become irritable and have to complete other tasks.
>
> d. Discuss with Bob the issues he is having with the system. Start a new training session at a much simpler level.

Scenario 10

You work in department that shares office space with others. Everyone in your department is given a new computer system and you are left out.

What should you do?

> a. Consider this as a small mistake and talk to the head of department.
>
> b. Confront the head of department and ask him to explain why you are being treated unfairly.
>
> c. Take a new computer from a colleague.
>
> d. Make a complaint with the HR department.

Scenario 11

You arrive at the scene of a fire and see a bystander trying to enter the building to rescue a trapped person. What should you do?

    a. Allow the bystander to go in, as they may know the person.

    b. Inform the bystander that it's too dangerous and prevent them from entering.

    c. Join the bystander and go in together to save the person.

    d. Call for backup while letting the bystander enter.

Scenario 12

While battling a fire in a residential area, an elderly neighbor approaches you, very distressed about their home. How do you respond?

    a. Tell the neighbor to calm down and stay back.

    b. Ignore the neighbor; focus on the fire.

    c. Reassure the neighbor that you're doing everything possible and ask for their address.

    d. Ask a fellow firefighter to deal with the neighbor while you continue fighting the fire.

Scenario 13

At a community event, a child asks you what to do if there's a fire. What is your best response?

    a. Tell the child to just run away as fast as possible.

    b. Explain fire safety tips in a way that's understandable for their age.

    c. Avoid answering as it's not appropriate for children.

    d. Say that you will handle it and they should not worry about it.

Scenario 14

You notice a fellow firefighter struggling with gear during a hectic situation. What should you do?

a. Continue with your tasks; they need to figure it out.

b. Yell at them to hurry up and focus.

c. Offer your assistance to help them get ready faster.

d. Report them to the chief for not being prepared.

Scenario 15

After extinguishing a fire, you find a distraught homeowner who is worried about their pets left inside. What do you do?

a. Tell them there's nothing you can do now.

b. Reassure them and check if it's safe to search for the pets.

c. Advise them to leave the site immediately.

d. Ignore the homeowner; your job is done.

Answer Key

1. B

The editor is your boss and that's the way things are so if they are not happy that will mean some adjustment on your part. However, if you feel the editor is being unreasonable, you may want to talk with them. Choice C, referring to the company policy document is a possibility depending on the situation.

Choice A, ignorance is no defense in any situation in life. By ignoring to address the concerns of the clients you set a pace for failure. You are bound to lose more clients. Choice D, blaming the supervisor will only lead to more complications. Building resentment and bad publicity are sure consequences of such behavior.

2. A

Division of labor and specialization are the best ways of solving increasing workload. This gives the employees equal time to work on given tasks to ease the workload. Division of labor pro-motes innovation and invention and increases output per employee.

3. A

First, discuss it with your colleague. There may be things you are not aware of preventing them from getting information to you quickly. If this doesn't work, go to the other options.

Choice B, going to your supervisor is an option for later. Choice C, is not a great approach. Making demands is not likely to change anything. Choice D, getting information from other sources would mean that there is a disharmony between the key participants. This may be an option for later or as a last resort.

4. D

The changes are going to continue so your choice is to resist (difficult) or become more involved. Once you are more involved in why the changes are taking place they become easier to manage.

5. D

Self-improvement is a continuous process and any person who can't handle feedback or criticism positively loses the opportunity to improve.

Choice A and C, retaliating against your critics or resenting, is destructive. You can't win an argument and even when you think you have, the resentment stirred in your victim works against you and your plans. Choice B, giving the matter to supervisors, may be a next step but not a good strategy initially.

6. C

Clear communication is vital in such a scenario as a first step. If this doesn't resolve the issue the other choices are next steps.

Incorrect answers B and D
Being bossy (choice B) leads to resentment. Choice D, requesting their supervisor intervene is a possible next step.

7. A

Verbal communication is not always the best because there is never proof of communication. The best way to communicate is through written communication. By following written communication, you are provided with evidence of communication for reference in future.

Choice B, refusing to consider verbal communication is too extreme. Choice D is incorrect be-cause you don't want to be complacent when communicating with others.

8. C

Some of the disagreements require input from higher authority. Supervisors are in a better position to resolve a conflict between junior employees.

Choice A is not a resolution. Choice B, confronting the behavior may work if done properly, but could also make the situation worse, however, choice C is the better choice. Choice D, motivating yourself could work towards making you feel better but not towards resolving the conflict.

9. A

It is the only approach when you search for the root of Bob's issues. Understanding what he finds challenging, you are showing strong listening skills. You often demonstrate adaptability by adjusting the solution to the issue. By being supportive and providing answers, you are a team player to improve the understanding of your colleague.

It might be more beneficial to let another worker with more expertise take over. However, your boss has assigned you this assignment, and it is not your duty to assign it to anyone else. Most likely, the issue does not rely on the degree of expertise but the method of teaching. You do not demonstrate the adaptability of your method of teaching by letting Anna teach him.

10. A

Choice A is the best response. If you have not been given the right tools and equipment to do your job, talking to your head of department or direct supervisor is the right move. It is the responsibility of your head of department to help ensure you have all it takes to do your job.

Jumping to conclusions that you have been treated unfairly or taking a new colleague's computer may prove embarrassing if it was a simple mistake.

11. B

It's important to prioritize safety. You should inform the bystander that entering the building is too dangerous. Firefighters are trained to handle such situations, and it's crucial to prevent untrained individuals from putting themselves in danger.

12. C

Reassuring the neighbor and asking for their address shows empathy and provides them with some comfort. It's essential to acknowledge people's feelings during emergencies, even while focusing on the task at hand.

13. B
Explaining fire safety tips in an age-appropriate manner helps educate the child and prepares them for emergencies. It's crucial to empower children with knowledge about fire safety rather than instilling fear.

14. C
Offering assistance fosters teamwork and helps ensure everyone is properly equipped to handle the emergency. Supporting each other is vital in high-pressure situations like fire fighting.

15. B
Reassuring the homeowner and checking if it's safe to search for the pets demonstrates compassion and responsibility. It's important to address the concerns of those affected by the incident whenever possible.

MAPPING

The mapping section is part of the mechanical aptitude and reasoning assessment. This evaluates yokur ability to understand and interpret maps, diagrams, and mechanical drawings.

Firefighters need these skills to navigate and make decisions during emergencies.

The questions below are not the same as you will find on the Gledhill Shaw exam - that would be too easy! And nobody knows what the questions will be and they change all the time. So, while the format and exact wording of the questions may differ, and change from year to year, if you can answer the questions below, you will have no problem with the mapping section.

Mapping Self-Assessment

```
     A   B   C   D
 1   ○   ○   ○   ○
 2   ○   ○   ○   ○
 3   ○   ○   ○   ○
 4   ○   ○   ○   ○
 5   ○   ○   ○   ○
 6   ○   ○   ○   ○
 7   ○   ○   ○   ○
 8   ○   ○   ○   ○
 9   ○   ○   ○   ○
10   ○   ○   ○   ○
```

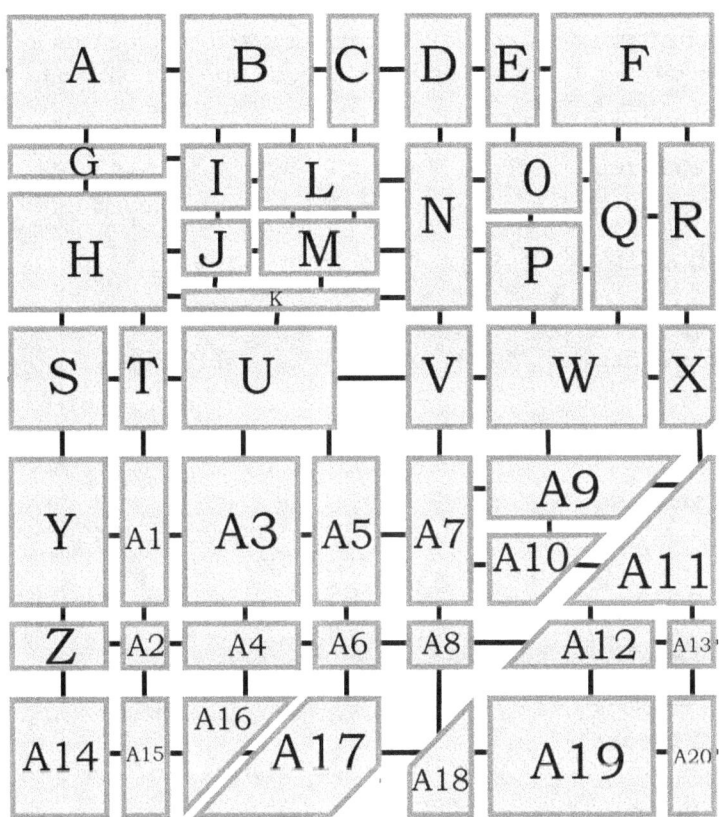

MAP KEY

Each square labeled A to Z and A1 to A20, represent the corner of an intersection. The lines between the squares represent a city block. The intersections and city blocks fall under 3 categories.

Large blocks: A, B,F, H, N, Q, R, U, W, Y, A3, A5, A7, A9, A11, A14, A17, A19

Small blocks: C, D, E, I. J, L,M, O, P, S, T, V, X, A1, A4, A10, Z, A12, A15, A16, A18, A20

Mini blocks: G, K, A2, A6, A8, A13

The time it takes to travel from one city block to another is:

Large blocks

    In a car: 4 minutes
    On a bike: 6 minutes
    On foot: 10 minutes

Small Blocks

    In a car: 3 minutes
    On a bike: 5 minutes
    On foot: 8 minutes

Mini Blocks

    In a car: 2 minutes
    On a bike: 4 minutes
    On foot: 6 minutes

6. What is the shortest time it would take a woman to go from block A to S driving a car?

   a. 11 minutes
   b. 7 and half minutes
   c. 8 minutes
   d. 10 minutes

7. What is the shortest time it would take a man to go from A to S if he drove the first two blocks, then rode a bike the rest of the way?

   a. 18 minutes
   b. 16 minutes
   c. 17 minutes
   d. 15 minutes

8. A student has to walk home from block U to R. What is the shortest time it would take him if he had to go through block Q?

   a. 38 minutes
   b. 32 minutes
   c. 37 minutes
   d. 29 minutes

9. A police patrol car in block Y has to respond to a call in Block G. How fast can they get there if they are forced by traffic to avoid Block S?

   a. 20 minutes
   b. 19 minutes
   c. 14 minutes
   d. 17 minutes

10. How fast would it take a man on bike to ride from block Z to block A7 if he had to spend two minutes and half along the way fixing his bike?

    a. 22. 5 minutes
    b. 22 minutes
    c. 24.5 minutes
    d. 24 minutes

Answer Key

6. D
The shortest route would take a car through A – G – H - S, covering two large blocks and one mini block. This would take 10 minutes by car.

7. B
The shortest route from A to S is A – G – H – S, taking 6 minutes by car for the first 2 blocks and 10 minutes on a bike for the last large block. Total time is 16 minutes.

8. A
The shortest route from U to R passing through Q is U – V – W – Q – R. Time to walk these blocks is 38 minutes. (A)

9. C
The shortest route from block Y to G, avoiding S, is Y – A1 – T – H – G. Time by car is 14 minutes.

10. C
The fastest route is Z – A2 – A4 – A6 – A8 – A7. Time by bike is 22 minutes, plus 2.5 minutes to fix the bike, for a total of 24.5 minutes.

Practice Test Questions Set 1

The practice test portion presents questions that are representative of the type of question you should expect to find on the Gledhill Shaw CPS Exam.

The questions here are for skill practice only.

For the best results, take this Practice Test as if it were the real exam. Set aside time when you will not be disturbed, and a location that is quiet and free of distractions. Read the instructions carefully, read each question carefully, and answer to the best of your ability.

Use the bubbles provided. When you have completed the Practice Test, check your answer against the Answer Key and read the explanation provided.

Reading Comprehension

	A	B	C	D	E		A	B	C	D	E
1	○	○	○	○	○	21	○	○	○	○	○
2	○	○	○	○	○	22	○	○	○	○	○
3	○	○	○	○	○	23	○	○	○	○	○
4	○	○	○	○	○	24	○	○	○	○	○
5	○	○	○	○	○	25	○	○	○	○	○
6	○	○	○	○	○	26	○	○	○	○	○
7	○	○	○	○	○	27	○	○	○	○	○
8	○	○	○	○	○	28	○	○	○	○	○
9	○	○	○	○	○	29	○	○	○	○	○
10	○	○	○	○	○	30	○	○	○	○	○
11	○	○	○	○	○						
12	○	○	○	○	○						
13	○	○	○	○	○						
14	○	○	○	○	○						
15	○	○	○	○	○						
16	○	○	○	○	○						
17	○	○	○	○	○						
18	○	○	○	○	○						
19	○	○	○	○	○						
20	○	○	○	○	○						

Listening Comprehension

	A	B	C	D
1	○	○	○	○
2	○	○	○	○
3	○	○	○	○
4	○	○	○	○
5	○	○	○	○
6	○	○	○	○
7	○	○	○	○
8	○	○	○	○
9	○	○	○	○
10	○	○	○	○
11	○	○	○	○
12	○	○	○	○
13	○	○	○	○
14	○	○	○	○
15	○	○	○	○
16	○	○	○	○
17	○	○	○	○
18	○	○	○	○
19	○	○	○	○
20	○	○	○	○

Mathematics

	A	B	C	D	E		A	B	C	D	E
1	○	○	○	○	○	21	○	○	○	○	○
2	○	○	○	○	○	22	○	○	○	○	○
3	○	○	○	○	○	23	○	○	○	○	○
4	○	○	○	○	○	24	○	○	○	○	○
5	○	○	○	○	○	25	○	○	○	○	○
6	○	○	○	○	○	26	○	○	○	○	○
7	○	○	○	○	○	27	○	○	○	○	○
8	○	○	○	○	○	28	○	○	○	○	○
9	○	○	○	○	○	29	○	○	○	○	○
10	○	○	○	○	○	30	○	○	○	○	○
11	○	○	○	○	○						
12	○	○	○	○	○						
13	○	○	○	○	○						
14	○	○	○	○	○						
15	○	○	○	○	○						
16	○	○	○	○	○						
17	○	○	○	○	○						
18	○	○	○	○	○						
19	○	○	○	○	○						
20	○	○	○	○	○						

Mechanical Aptitude

	A	B	C	D
1	○	○	○	○
2	○	○	○	○
3	○	○	○	○
4	○	○	○	○
5	○	○	○	○
6	○	○	○	○
7	○	○	○	○
8	○	○	○	○
9	○	○	○	○
10	○	○	○	○
11	○	○	○	○
12	○	○	○	○
13	○	○	○	○
14	○	○	○	○
15	○	○	○	○
16	○	○	○	○
17	○	○	○	○
18	○	○	○	○
19	○	○	○	○
20	○	○	○	○

Practice Test Questions 1

Mapping

	A	B	C	D
1	○	○	○	○
2	○	○	○	○
3	○	○	○	○
4	○	○	○	○
5	○	○	○	○
6	○	○	○	○
7	○	○	○	○
8	○	○	○	○
9	○	○	○	○
10	○	○	○	○
11	○	○	○	○
12	○	○	○	○
13	○	○	○	○
14	○	○	○	○
15	○	○	○	○

Situation Judgment

	A	B	C	D
1	○	○	○	○
2	○	○	○	○
3	○	○	○	○
4	○	○	○	○
5	○	○	○	○
6	○	○	○	○
7	○	○	○	○
8	○	○	○	○
9	○	○	○	○
10	○	○	○	○
11	○	○	○	○
12	○	○	○	○
13	○	○	○	○
14	○	○	○	○
15	○	○	○	○

Reading Comprehension

Directions: The following questions are based on several reading passages. Each passage is followed by a series of questions. Read each passage carefully, and then answer the questions based on it. You may reread the passage as often as you wish. When you have finished answering the questions based on one passage, go right onto the next passage. Choose the best answer based on the information given and implied.

Questions 1 – 4 refer to the following passage.

Firefighters are on call 24 hours a day, 7 days a week, 365 days a year - even on Christmas day! They provide an essential service in all countries. A firefighter's job can be quite tedious on-call, and then very stressful when responding to an emergency. They are responsible for attaching hoses to hydrants, using powerful pumps, as well as "flying" up ladders, and using various tools to break through windows and doors. A firefighter's duties also include entering burning buildings to rescue victims. Some firefighters are trained for providing on-site medical attention. Research conducted by the National Fire Protection Association, suggests most calls firefighters respond to are medical emergencies, and not fires. Firefighters perform other rescue tasks such as rescuing animals from trees.

Firefighters have to be very well rounded and capable of conducting a variety of tasks at the scene of an emergency. Some firefighters require forensic skills to determine the cause of a fire. A firefighters' duties may vary a lot of times while at the scene of an emergency. In some instances, they have to remain at the scene of a disaster for weeks, freeing trapped victims and providing medical assistance.

While at the station, firefighters are on-call always. During this time, they inspect equipment, conduct drills to stay sharp, as well as eat and sleep during a 24 hour shift.

There are different types of fires hence the need or different types of firefighters. Some of the various types of fire fighters include forest, structural, aircraft and shipboard firefighters.

Forest firefighters, also called Wildland Firefighters, use a variety of heavy equipment along with water hoses to tame forest fires. They often create fire lines which control the fire by starving it of fuel. There is a special team of firefighters called smoke jumpers who parachute from airplanes to target hard to reach areas of forest fires.

1. Which paragraph best summarizes the job of firefighters?

    a. First paragraph

    b. Third paragraph

    c. Fourth paragraph

    d. Last paragraph

2. Under which category of firefighters would you place smoke jumpers?

    a. Structural

    b. Shipboard

    c. Forest

    d. Air craft

3. What is the aim of this passage?

    a. To show that fire fighters work throughout the year

    b. Outlines the work of fire fighters

    c. Highlight the different types of firefighters

    d. All of the above

4. Which of the following are firefighters mostly called to respond to?

    a. Rescue animals
    b. Putting out fires
    c. Medical emergencies
    d. Carrying out search and rescue

Questions 5 – 8 refer to the following passage.

Low Blood Sugar

As the name suggest, low blood sugar is low sugar levels in the bloodstream. This can occur when you have not eaten properly and undertake strenuous activity, or, when you are very hungry. When Low blood sugar occurs regularly and is ongoing, it is a medical condition called hypoglycemia. This condition can occur in diabetics and in healthy adults.

Causes of low blood sugar can include excessive alcohol consumption, metabolic problems, stomach surgery, pancreas, liver or kidneys problems, as well as a side-effect of some medications.

Symptoms

There are different symptoms depending on the severity of the case.

Mild hypoglycemia can lead to feelings of nausea and hunger. The patient may also feel nervous, jittery and have fast heart beats. Sweaty skin, clammy and cold skin are likely symptoms.

Moderate hypoglycemia can result in short tempered-ness, confusion, nervousness, fear and blurring of vision. The patient may feel weak and unsteady.

Severe cases of hypoglycemia can lead to seizures, coma, fainting spells, nightmares, headaches, excessive sweats and severe tiredness.

Diagnosis of low blood sugar

A doctor can diagnosis this medical condition by asking the patient questions and testing blood and urine samples. Home testing kits are available for patients to monitor blood sugar levels. It is important to see a qualified doctor though. A doctor can administer tests to safely rule out other medical conditions that could affect blood sugar levels.

Treatment

Quick treatments include drinking or eating foods and drinks with high sugar contents. Good examples include soda, fruit juice, hard candy and raisins. Glucose energy tablets can also help. Doctors may also recommend medications and well as changes in diet and exercise routine to treat chronic low blood sugar.

5. Based on the article, which of the following is true?

    a. Low blood sugar can happen to anyone.

    b. Low blood sugar only happens to diabetics.

    c. Low blood sugar can occur even.

    d. None of the statements are true.

6. Which of the following are the author's opinion?

    a. Quick treatments include drinking or eating foods and drinks with high sugar contents.

    b. None of the statements are opinions.

    c. This condition can occur in diabetics and in healthy adults.

    d. There are different symptoms depending on the severity of the case

7. What is the author's purpose?

   a. To inform
   b. To persuade
   c. To entertain
   d. To analyze

8. Which of the following is not a detail?

   a. A doctor can diagnosis this medical condition by asking the patient questions and testing.
   b. A doctor will test blood and urine samples.
   c. Glucose energy tablets can also help.
   d. Home test kits monitor blood sugar levels.

Questions 9 - 12 refer to the following passage.

Passage 2 - When a Poet Longs to Mourn, He Writes an Elegy

Poems are an expressive, especially emotional, form of writing. They have been in literature virtually from the time civilizations invented the written word. Poets often portrayed as moody, secluded, and even troubled, but this is because poets are introspective and feel deeply about the current events and cultural norms they are surrounded with. Poets often produce the most telling literature, giving insight into the society and mind-set they come from. This can be done in many forms.

The oldest types of poems often include many stanzas, may or may not rhyme, and are more about telling a story than experimenting with language or words. The most common types of ancient poetry are epics, which are usually extremely long stories that follow a hero through his journey, or elegies, which are often solemn in tone and used to mourn or lament something or someone. The Mesopotamians are often said to have invented the written word, and their literature is among the oldest in the world, including the epic poem titled "Epic of Gilgamesh." Similar in style and length to "Gilgamesh" is "Beowulf," an elegy poem written in Old English and set in Scandinavia. These poems are often used by professors as the earliest examples of literature.

The importance of poetry was revived in the Renaissance. At this time, Europeans discovered the style and beauty of ancient Greek arts, and poetry was among those. Shakespeare is the most well-known poet of the time, and he used poetry not only to write poems but also to write plays for the theater. The most popular forms of poetry during the Renaissance included villanelles (a nineteen-line poem with two rhymes throughout), sonnets, as well as the epic. Poets during this time focused on style and form, and developed very specific rules and outlines for how an exceptional poem should be written.

As often happens in the arts, modern poets have rejected the constricting rules of Renaissance poets, and free form poems are much more popular. Some modern poems would read just like stories if they weren't arranged into lines and stanzas. It is difficult to tell which poems and poets will be the most important, because works of art often become more famous in hindsight, after the poet has died and society can look at itself without being in the moment. Modern poetry continues to develop, and will no doubt continue to change as values, thought, and writing continue to change.

Poems can be among the most enlightening and uplifting texts for a person to read if they are looking to connect with the past, connect with other people, or try to gain an understanding of what is happening in their time.

9. In summary, the author has written this passage

    a. as a foreword that will introduce a poem in a book or magazine

    b. because she loves poetry and wants more people to like it

    c. to give a brief history of poems

    d. to convince students to write poems

10. The author organizes the paragraphs mainly by

a. moving chronologically, explaining which types of poetry were common in that time

b. talking about new types of poems each paragraph and explaining them a little

c. focusing on one poet or group of people and the poems they wrote

d. explaining older types of poetry so she can talk about modern poetry

11. The author's claim that poetry has been around "virtually from the time civilizations invented the written word" is supported by the detail that

a. Beowulf is written in Old English, which is not really in use any longer

b. epic poems told stories about heroes

c. the Renaissance poets tried to copy Greek poets

d. the Mesopotamians are credited with both inventing the word and writing "Epic of Gilgamesh"

12. According to the passage, the word "telling" means

a. speaking

b. significant

c. soothing

d. wordy

Questions 13 – 15 refer to the following passage.

Passage 4 If You Have Allergies, You're Not Alone

People who experience allergies might joke that their immune systems have let them down or are seriously lacking. Truthfully though, people who experience allergic reactions or allergy symptoms during certain times of the year have heightened immune systems that are "better" than those of people who have perfectly healthy but less militant immune systems.

Still, when a person has an allergic reaction, they are having an adverse reaction to a substance that is considered normal to most people. Mild allergic reactions usually have symptoms like itching, runny nose, red eyes, or bumps or discoloration of the skin. More serious allergic reactions, such as those to animal and insect poisons or certain foods, may result in the closing of the throat, swelling of the eyes, low blood pressure, an inability to breath, and can even be fatal.

Different treatments help different allergies, and depend on the nature and severity of the allergy. It is recommended to patients with severe allergies to take extra precautions, such as carrying an EpiPen, which treats anaphylactic shock and may prevent death, always in order for the remedy to be readily available and more effective. When an allergy is not so severe, treatments may be used just relieve a person of uncomfortable symptoms. Over the counter allergy medicines treat milder symptoms, and can be bought at any grocery store and used in moderation to help people with allergies live normally.

There are many tests available to assess whether a person has allergies or what they may be allergic to, and advances in these tests and the medicine used to treat patients continues to improve. Despite this fact, allergies still affect many people throughout the year or even every day. Medicines used to treat allergies have side-effects, and it is difficult to bring the body into balance with the use of medicine. Regardless, many of those who live with allergies are grateful for what is available and find it useful in maintaining their lifestyles.

13. According to this passage, which group does the word "militant" belong in

    a. sickly, ailing, faint

    b. strength, power, vigor

    c. active, fighting, warring

    d. worn, tired, breaking down

14. The author says that "medicines used to treat allergies have side-effects" to

    a. point out that doctors aren't very good at diagnosing and treating allergies

    b. argue that because of the large number of people with allergies, a cure will never be found

    c. explain that allergy medicines aren't cures and some compromise must be made

    d. argue that more wholesome remedies should be researched and medicines banned

15. It can be inferred that _____ recommend that some people with allergies carry medicine with them.

    a. the author

    b. doctors

    c. the makers of EpiPen

    d. people with allergies

Questions 16 - 19 refer to the following passage.

Winged Victory of Samothrace: the Statue of the Gods

Students who read about the "Winged Victory of Samothrace" probably won't be able to picture what this statue looks like. However, almost anyone who knows a little about statues will recognize it when they see it: it is the statue of a winged woman who does not have arms or a head. Even the most famous pieces of art may be recognized by sight but not by name.

This iconic statue is of the Greek goddess Nike, who represented victory and was called Victoria by the Romans. The statue is sometimes called the "Nike of Samothrace." She was often displayed in Greek art as driving a chariot, and her speed or efficiency with the chariot may be what her wings symbolize. It is said that the statue was created around 200 BCE to celebrate a battle that was won at sea. Archaeologists and art historians believe the statue may have originally been part of a temple or other building, even one of the most important temples, Megaloi Theoi, just as many statues were used during that time.

"Winged Victory" does indeed appear to have had arms and a head when it was originally created, and it is unclear why they were removed or lost. Indeed, they have never been discovered, even with all the excavation that has taken place. Many speculate that one of her arms was raised and put to her mouth, as though she was shouting or calling out, which is consistent with the idea of her as a war figure. If the missing pieces were ever to be found, they might give Greek and art historians more of an idea of what Nike represented or how the statue was used. Learning about pieces of art through details like these can help students remember time frames or locations, as well as learn about the people who occupied them.

16. The author's title says the statue is "of the Gods" because

    a. the statue is very beautiful and even a god would find it beautiful

    b. the statue is of a Greek goddess, and gods were of primary importance to the Greek

    c. Nike lead the gods into war

    d. the statues were used at the temple of the gods and so it belonged to them

17. The third paragraph states that

    a. the statue is related to war and was probably broken apart by foreign soldiers

    b. the arms and head of the statue cannot be found because all the excavation has taken place

    c. speculations have been made about what the entire statue looked like and what it symbolized

    d. the statue has no arms or head because the sculptor lost them

18. The author's main purpose in writing this passage is to

    a. demonstrate that art and culture are related and one can teach us about the other

    b. persuade readers to become archaeologists and find the missing pieces of the statue

    c. teach readers about the Greek goddess Nike

    d. to teach readers the name of a statue they probably recognize

19. The author specifies the indirect audience as "students" because

    a. it is probably a student who is taking this test

    b. most young people don't know much about art yet and most young people are students

    c. students read more than people who are not students

    d. the passage is based on a discussion of what we can learn about culture from art

Questions 20 - 22 refer to the following passage.

Fires can be useful, deadly, destructive it all depends whether or not you can control it. There was a time when I thought that all fires could be extinguished with water, but boy was I wrong and I learned the hard way too. My father is an electrician and a pretty good one too, I remember he was working in the garage one day and just like that an electrical fire had started. I ran to get a bucket of water and swiftly threw it on the fire. Not only did the fire burn my father bet he also suffered electrical shocks. Little did I know that electrical fires can't be extinguished like that.

There are several different types of fires and they can't all be extinguished in the same way. While most fires can be extinguished using water, many require different means to be extinguished. Memory takes me back to a grade nine science class on combustion, when the teacher poured gasoline on the surface of water in a beaker, then lit it with a match. The fire walked on the surface of the water. I though this was impossible and even stated this in my hypothesis before the experiment. The teacher then covered the beaker with a piece of cardboard. I thought the fire would burn through the cardboard, but instead it went out. It was then explained that fire requires oxygen, fuel and heat to burn. When the oxygen is removed, the fire goes out.

There are many types of fire extinguishers on the market. Water and Foam extinguishers that snuffs out a fire by removing the heat from the fire; Carbon Dioxide fire extinguishers that put out fires by removing oxygen (fuel)

from the fire. Dry Chemical fire extinguishers put out fires by disrupting the chemical reaction taking place in the fire. Dry Powder extinguishers work by separating the fuel from the oxygen or by removing heat from the fire.

Scientist are also constantly formulating new ways of putting out fires. Since 2015 a set of university students have discovered that even sound waves can extinguish fires.

20. What is a new way to extinguish fire being studied?

    a. Sound

    b. Liquid oxygen

    c. Light

    d. All of the above

21. The purpose of the article is to

    a. Highlight ways of extinguishing fires

    b. Highlight the different types of fire extinguishers on the market

    c. Provide information on fires

    d. Distinguish between different types of fires

22. Which type of fire should NOT be extinguished by water?

    a. Forest fires

    b. Fires with gasoline as the fuel

    c. Electrical fires

    d. None of the above

Questions 23 – 26 refer to the following passage.

Ways Characters Communicate in Theater

Playwrights give their characters voices in a way that gives depth and added meaning to what happens on stage during their play. There are different types of speech in scripts that allow characters to talk with themselves, with other characters, and even with the audience.

It is very unique to theater that characters may talk "to themselves." When characters do this, the speech they give is called a soliloquy. Soliloquies are usually poetic, introspective, moving, and can tell audience members about the feelings, motivations, or suspicions of an individual character without that character having to reveal them to other characters on stage. "To be or not to be" is a famous soliloquy given by Hamlet as he considers difficult but important themes, such as life and death.

The most common type of communication in plays is when one character is speaking to another or a group of other characters. This is generally called dialogue, but can also be called monologue if one character speaks without being interrupted for a long time. It is not necessarily the most important type of communication, but it is the most common because the plot of the play cannot really progress without it.

Lastly, and most unique to theater (although it has been used somewhat in film) is when a character speaks directly to the audience. This is called an aside, and scripts usually specifically direct actors to do this. Asides are usually comical, an inside joke between the character and the audience, and very short. The actor will usually face the audience when delivering them, even if it's for a moment, so the audience can recognize this move as an aside.

All three of these types of communication are important to the art of theater, and have been perfected by famous playwrights like Shakespeare. Understanding these types of communication can help an audience member grasp what is artful about the script and action of a play.

23. According to the passage, characters in plays communicate to

a. move the plot forward

b. show the private thoughts and feelings of one character

c. make the audience laugh

d. add beauty and artistry to the play

24. When Hamlet delivers "To be or not to be," he can be described as

a. solitary

b. thoughtful

c. dramatic

d. hopeless

25. The author uses parentheses to punctuate "although it has been used somewhat in film"

a. to show that films are less important

b. instead of using commas so that the sentence is not interrupted

c. because parenthesis help separate details that are not as important

d. to show that films are not as artistic

26. What does the author mean by the phrase "give their characters voices?"

a. playwrights are generous

b. playwrights are changing the sound or meaning of characters' voices to fit what they had in mind

c. dialogue is important in creating characters

d. playwrights may be the parent of one of their actors and literally give them their voice

27. Consider the gauge above. What PSI is the limit of the safe working range?

    a. About 80 PSI
    b. About 90 PSI
    c. About 60 PSI
    d. About 100 PSI

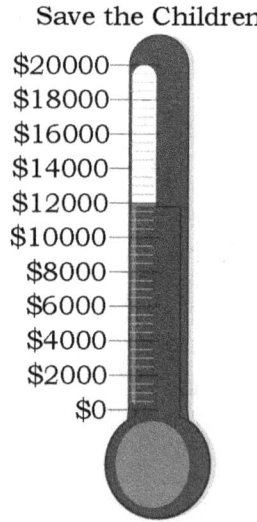

28. Consider the graphic above. The Save the Children fund has a fund-raising goal of $20,000. About how much of their goal have they achieved?

   a. 3/5
   b. 3/4
   c. 1/2
   d. 1/3

Questions 29 – 30 refer to the following passage.

The Life of a Firefighter

The life of a firefighter is pretty hectic, we are always on call, always training, always conducting drills and working 24 hours shift each day. "We practically live at work," as a colleague of mine puts it. Fires, like hurricanes are largely unpredictable, although they do have a season. The dry season always keeps us on our toes, and on some days we have to respond to simultaneous emergencies. On one particular day last week, putting out a fire in a warehouse was going smoothly, a hydrant was nearby, and the fire was almost under control. However, as we advanced into the building, we stumbled on an unconscious victim. I frenetically dashed towards the victim while my colleagues continued tackling the fire.

As firefighters, we are instinctively confident persons, however overconfidence can create complacency. I often make reference to the scenario mentioned above and pose the question: how would you respond? The unanimous response is usually, "get the victim and evacuate." This may sound plausible, however in the real world, it's not so simple; you may encounter another victim, or you can't go back the way you came, or you may get injured in the process. Therefore, grabbing an unconscious body and getting the person to safety is anything but simple.

During training sessions, the "casualties" are usually lifeless dummies that could never imitate the feel of an actual unconscious person, or the "casualties" are other colleagues who are usually very healthy. As firefighters, we must also be aware that environmental factors such as heat, smoke, and the lack of visibility may render some of the techniques we take for granted impractical or even harmful to the victim.

Most fires do not have casualties. This is due to upgrades in building construction, as well as easier and clearly marked exits to safely evacuate buildings. In addition, fire extinguishers are common and required by most building codes. As well, there is greater public awareness about fires and how to respond in an emergency has substantially reduced the number of casualties.

29. Why are fires compared to hurricanes?

    a. Both fires and hurricanes are devastating

    b. To show the destructive power of fires

    c. To show that fires are equally as powerful as hurricanes

    d. Both fires and hurricanes are unpredictable

30. According to the narrator, what may cause complacency among firefighters?

    a. Lack of confidence

    b. Overconfidence

    c. Overly preparedness

    d. Lack of training

Listening Comprehension

Directions: Scan the QR code below with any smartphone or tablet for an audio recording of the listening comprehension passages below. Or, have someone read them to you. Listen carefully to the passages and answer the questions that follow.

What is a QR Code?
A QR code looks like a barcode and it's used as a shortcut to link to content online using your phone's camera, saving you from typing lengthy addresses into your mobile browser.

Questions 8 – 11 refer to the following passage.

Fire Extinguishers

Fire extinguishers are used to put out or prevent small fires that are unexpected or accidental and has not reached the maximum burning potential and is controllable.

Fire extinguishers are placed in all buildings like companies, offices, government corporations and most people's homes. These extinguishers are serviced by a fire protection service company at least every year. Regular servicing is essential to prevent the unfortunate possibility they will be unavailable when really needed. Service companies provide services like, checking whether there is any replacement of the device needed as well as any recharging power.

Fire extinguishers can be handheld or cart-mounted, also called wheeled extinguisher. These two extinguishers have differences in weights. Handheld extinguishers weigh much less than cart-mounted extinguishers. Handheld generally weigh anywhere from 1 to 30 lbs., while cart-mounted extinguishers weigh more than 50 lbs. Wheel models are commonly found at construction sites, airport runways, heliports and docks.

Scan for Audio or click
https://www.test-preparation.ca/audio/FireExtinguishers.wav

1. What types of fires are extinguishers NOT intended for?

    a. Electrical fires

    b. Out of control fires

    c. Fires on a boat or marina

    d. None of the above

2. How often are fire extinguishers inspected?

    a. Every 6 months

    b. There is no set time

    c. Every year

    d. Every 5 years

3. What are the two types of fire extinguishers?

    a. Stored pressure and cartridge-operated

    b. Chemical and water based

    c. Chemical and gas such as CO_2

    d. None of the above

4. About how much do hand-held fire extinguishers weigh?

    a. 20 pounds

    b. 1 - 30 pounds

    c. 10 pounds

    d. 50 pounds

Questions 5 – 8 refer to the following passage.

Flame

Flames are the visible gaseous part of the fire. Flames have a wide range of colors and temperatures, which depends on the type of fuel. Fire continues to burn in a chain reaction that feeds on itself. The heat from the fire reaction vaporizes fuel molecules, which react with oxygen, creating more heat.

Incomplete combustion, generally of organic matter, produces an orange flame, releases less energy and produces carbon monoxide which is a poisonous gas.

When the combustion of a gas is complete the flame is blue.

The color of the flame, as well as the temperature, and therefore the rate of combustion depend on the fuel and oxygen supply mix.

Many combustion reactions do not require a flame, such as the reaction in an internal combustion engine. Various ways are used to eliminate a flame in combustion engines depending on the type of fuel.

Scan for audio or click
https://www.test-preparation.ca/audio/Flame-2.mp3

5. Under what conditions is a flame orange-red?

    a. Flames are always orange red

    b. Flames are orange red when burning non-organic matter

    c. Burning organic matter and the incomplete combustion of gas

    d. None of the above

6. When are flames blue?

  a. When the gases are not completely combusted
  b. When the gases are complete combusted
  c. When burning non-organic matter
  d. None of the above

7. Is oxygen always present for a flame to burn?

  a. Yes
  b. No

8. What color is the flame in combustion engines?

  a. Red
  b. Orange
  c. White
  d. There is no flame in combustion engines

Questions 9 – 11 refer to the following passage.

Fire

Fire has both positive and negative effects for humans as well as ecosystems. Fire is used for food preparations, providing heat for warmth, light, smoke is often a sign of danger.

Forest fires have a major impact on ecosystems, restoring and rejuvenating by turning dead trees and decaying plant matters into ashes and returning nutrients into the soil. Atmospheric pollution from fire has a major negative effect on the environment. Air pollution from fire and combustion kills millions of people every year worldwide.

Scan for audio or click
https://www.test-preparation.ca/audio/Fire-3.mp3

9. What are some positive effects of fire?

    a. heat, light and smoke

    b. Returning dead trees to the soil

    c. Restoring nutrients to the soil

    d. None of the above

10. What are some positive effects of fire on the ecosystem?

    a. Rejuvenating the soil

    b. Providing heat and warmth

    c. Warning of danger

    c. None of the above

11. What is a major negative effect of fire?

    a. Signalling danger

    b. Returning dead trees to the soil

    c. Air Pollution

    d. None of the above

Questions 12 - 14 refer to the following passage.

Insects

Insects were the first animals able to fly. Most, but not all insects have wings, and all have six legs. Their life-cycle varies but most hatch eggs. Insects undergo a transformation process, called metamorphosis, where the immature insects undergo two or three stages. Insects outgrow their bodies and shed, or molt their old body several times.

Adult insects walk, sometimes swim, or fly.

Most insects have a walking style called tripedal. In this walking style or gait, their six legs touch the ground in alternating triangles. This gait allows for very rapid movement. Insects are mostly solitary but some, such as ants or bees live in colonies. Even though insect colonies have hundreds of individuals, they function together as one organism.

Insects are found all over the world, in virtually every environment. A few even live in the ocean. Some insects feed on fruit and crops and are classified as pests, and controlled with pesticides and other means. Others perform complex ecological roles and some spread disease.

Insects communicate in a variety of ways. For example, some insects, like crickets, produce a sound, by rubbing their legs together. Some beetles communicate with light.

Scan for audio or click
https://www.test-preparation.ca/audio/Insects-3.mp3

12. Choose the correct sentence.

   a. No insects can swim.

   b. All insects are excellent swimmers.

   c. Some insects are excellent swimmers.

   d. Most insects are excellent swimmers.

13. Choose the correct sentence.

   a. All insects communicate with sound.

   b. No insects communicate with sound.

   c. Insects don't communicate

   d. Many insects communicate with sound.

14. Are insects solitary or social?

   a. Solitary

   b. Social

   c. Some are social and some are solitary

   d. None of the above

Questions 15 - 16 refer to the following passage.

Trees

Trees are essential part of our natural ecosystem and provide shelter, fuel, medicine and much more. One of the principal benefits of trees is the photosynthesis process where carbon dioxide is absorbed, and oxygen released. Trees are also important in preventing erosion. Trees remove many types of pollutants in addition to carbon dioxide.

Trees have many practical applications. Wood is a fuel for heat as well as cooking for much of the world. Timber is used for construction, and pulp from wood is used to make paper.

Tree bark provides important medicines such as aspirin and quinine.

Scan for audio or click
https://www.test-preparation.ca/audio/Trees-3.mp3

15. What are two reasons trees are important in the natural landscape?

    a. They prevent erosion and produce oxygen.

    b. They produce fruit and are important elements in c. landscaping.

    c. Trees are not important in the natural landscape.

    d. Trees produce carbon dioxide and prevent erosion.

16. What do trees do to the atmosphere?

    a. Trees produce carbon dioxide and reduce oxygen.

    b. Trees produce oxygen and carbon dioxide.

    c. Trees reduce oxygen and carbon dioxide.

    d. Trees produce oxygen and reduce carbon dioxide.

Questions 17 - 20 refer to the following passage.

Fire Fighters

Firefighters are trained to put out any type of fire and perform many types of rescues. There are fire departments in almost every country in the world. Firefighters are one of the three main emergency services, along with the police department and the emergency medical services.

Firefighters receive extensive training in fire fighting to assure that they are prepared to handle any situation. While on duty, firemen or firewomen might have to deal with fire prevention, fire suppression, ventilation, containment, search and rescue, and many other situations.

The main goal of the fire departments is to save lives, protect property, and protect the environment from the dangers of fires. Traditionally, the firefighters are associated with Dalmatians as helper animals. While most fire departments use dogs, they are not Dalmatians. Fire departments only used dogs for rescue operations, and keep them away from fires.

Scan for Audio or click
https://www.test-preparation.ca/audio/Firefighters.mp3

17. What are the three main emergency services?

    a. Fire departments, emergency medical and police

    b. Fire departments, emergency medical and highway patrol

    c. RCMP, fire departments and emergency medical

    d. Disaster relief, fire departments, and emergency medical

18. What are the main goals of the fire department?

    a. Put out fires and protect property

    b. To save lives, protect property and protect the environment

    c. To save lives, put out fires and protect property

    d. To protect property, save the environment and put out fires

19. What animal is traditionally associated with firefighters?

    a. Dogs

    b. Dalmatians

    c. Horses

    d. No animal

20. Do animals assist firefighters putting out fires?

    a. Yes

    b. No

    c. The articles doesn't say.

Mathematics

1. What is 1/3 of 3/4?

    a. 1/4

    b. 1/3

    c. 2/3

    d. 3/4

2. What fraction of $1500 is $75?

   a. 1/14
   b. 3/5
   c. 7/10
   d. 1/20

3. 3.14 + 2.73 + 23.7 =

   a. 28.57
   b. 30.57
   c. 29.56
   d. 29.57

4. A woman spent 15% of her income on an item and ends with $120. What percentage of her income is left?

   a. 12%
   b. 85%
   c. 75%
   d. 95%

5. Express 0.27 + 0.33 as a fraction.

   a. 3/6
   b. 4/7
   c. 3/5
   d. 2/7

6. What is (3.13 + 7.87) X 5?

   a. 65
   b. 50
   c. 45
   d. 55

7. Reduce 2/4 X 3/4 to lowest terms.

    a. 6/12
    b. 3/8
    c. 6/16
    d. 3/4

8. 2/3 − 2/5 =

    a. 4/10
    b. 1/15
    c. 3/7
    d. 4/15

9. 2/7 + 2/3 =

    a. 12/23
    b. 5/10
    c. 20/21
    d. 6/21

10. 2/3 of 60 + 1/5 of 75 =

    a. 45
    b. 55
    c. 15
    d. 50

11. 8 is what percent of 40?

    a. 10%
    b. 15%
    c. 20%
    d. 25%

12. 9 is what percent of 36?

   a. 10%
   b. 15%
   c. 20%
   d. 25%

13. Three tenths of 90 equals:

   a. 18
   b. 45
   c. 27
   d. 36

14. .4% of 36 is

   a. .144
   b. 1.44
   c. 14.4
   d. 144

15. Convert 0.007 kilograms to grams

   a. 7 grams
   b. 70 grams
   c. 0.07 grams
   d. 0.70 grams

16. Convert 16 quarts to gallons

   a. 1 gallons
   b. 8 gallons
   c. 4 gallons
   d. 4.5 gallons

17. Convert 200 meters to kilometers

    a. 50 kilometers
    b. 20 kilometers
    c. 12 kilometers
    d. 0.2 kilometers

18. Convert 72 inches to feet

    a. 12 feet
    b. 6 feet
    c. 4 feet
    d. 17 feet

19. Convert 3 yards to feet

    a. 18 feet
    b. 12 feet
    c. 9 feet
    d. 27 feet

20. Convert 45 kg. to pounds.

    a. 10 pounds
    b. 100 pounds
    c. 1,000 pounds
    d. 110 pounds

21. Convert 0.63 grams to mg.

    a. 630 g.
    b. 63 mg.
    c. 630 mg.
    d. 603 mg.

22. The price of a book went up from $20 to $25. What percent did the price increase?

    a. 5%
    b. 10%
    c. 20%
    d. 25%

23. The price of a book decreased from $25 to $20. What percent did the price decrease?

    a. 5%
    b. 10%
    c. 20%
    d. 25%

24. After taking several practice tests, Brian improved the results of his GRE test by 30%. Given that the first time he took the test, he answered 150 questions correctly, how many questions did he answer correctly the second time?

    a. 105
    b. 120
    c. 180
    d. 195

25. On a local baseball team, 4 players (or 12.5% of the team) have long hair and the rest have short hair. How many short-haired players are there on the team?

    a. 24
    b. 28
    c. 32
    d. 50

26. In the time required to serve 43 customers, a server breaks 2 glasses and slips 5 times. The next day, the same server breaks 10 glasses. Assuming the number of glasses broken is proportional to the number of customers, how many customers did she serve?

    a. 25
    b. 43
    c. 86
    d. 215

27. A square lawn has an area of 62,500 square meters. What will the cost of building fence around it at a rate of $5.5 per meter?

    a. $4000
    b. $4500
    c. $5000
    d. $5500

28. Mr. Brown bought 5 cheese burgers, 3 drinks, and 4 fries for his family, and a cookie pack for his dog. If the price of all single items is the same at $1.30 and a 3.5% tax is added, what is the total cost of dinner for Mr. Brown?

    a. $16
    b. $16.9
    c. $17
    d. $17.5

29. A distributor purchased 550 kilograms of potatoes for $165. He distributed these at a rate of $6.4 per 20 kilograms to 15 shops, $3.4 per 10 kilograms to 12 shops and the remainder at $1.8 per 5 kilograms. If his total distribution cost is $10, what will his profit be?

    a. $10.40

    b. $8.60

    c. $14.90

    d. $23.40

30. How much pay does Mr. Johnson receive if he gives half of his pay to his family, $250 to his landlord, and has exactly 3/7 of his pay left over?

    a. $3600

    b. $3500

    c. $2800

    d. $1750

Mechanical Comprehension

1. What is mechanical advantage?

    a. The ratio of energy input to energy output, typically where the input is less than the output.

    b. The ratio of energy input to energy output, typically where the input is greater than the output.

    c. The ratio of energy resistance to energy output, typically where the resistance is less than the output.

    d. None of the above

2. What is the ratio of mechanical advantage of a simple pulley?

    a. 2:1

    b. 1:1

    c. 3:1

    d. 1:2

3. Consider moving an object with a lever and a fulcrum. What is the relationship between the distance from the fulcrum and the speed the object will move?

    a. The farther away from the fulcrum, the faster the object will move.

    b. The closer to the fulcrum, the faster an object will move.

    c. An object will move the fastest when directly above the fulcrum.

    d. None of the above.

4. Which of the following are examples of a wedge?

    a. Corkscrew

    b. Scissors

    c. Wheelbarrow

    d. Pulley

5. Which of the following illustrates the principle of the lever?

    a. The greater the distance over which the force is applied, the greater the force required (to lift the load).

    b. The greater the distance over which the force is applied, the smaller the force required (to lift the load).

    c. The smaller the distance over which the force is applied, the smaller the force required (to lift the load).

    d. None of the above

6. Consider two gears on separate shafts that mesh. The input gear has 30 teeth and turns at 100 rpm. If the output gear has 40 teeth, how fast is the output gear turning?

   a. 300 rpm
   b. 250 rpm
   c. 75 rpm
   d. 100 rpm

7. Consider two gears on separate shafts that mesh. The input gear has 100 teeth and turns at 50 rpm. If the output gear has 20 teeth, how fast is the output gear turning?

   a. 300 rpm
   b. 250 rpm
   c. 200 rpm
   d. 100 rpm

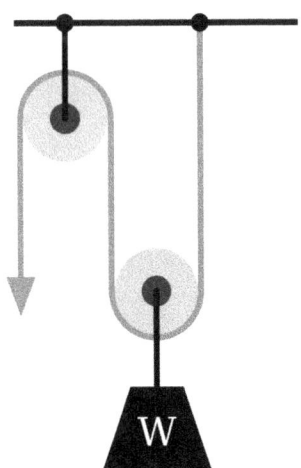

8. Consider the pulley arrangement above. If the weight is 100 pounds, how much force is required to lift it?

   a. 20 pounds
   b. 33 pounds
   c. 50 pounds
   d. 75 pounds

9. What type of screwdriver is used with the screw pictured above?

   a. Robertson
   b. Slot
   c. Philips
   d. Hex

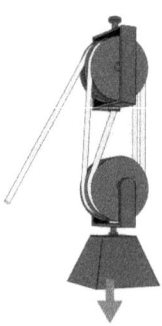

10. Consider the pulley arrangement above. If the weight is 200 pounds, how much force must be exerted downward on the rope?

   a. 200 pounds
   b. 100 pounds
   c. 50 pounds
   d. 25 pounds

11. Up-and-down or back-and-forth motion is called:

   a. Rotary motion
   b. Reciprocating motion
   c. Agitation motion
   d. Harmonic motion

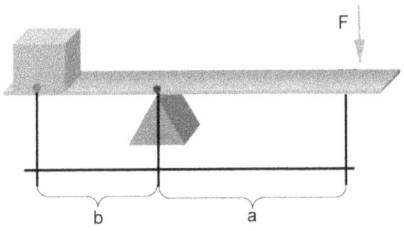

12. Consider the illustration above and the corresponding data:

Weight = W = 80 pounds
Distance from fulcrum to Weight = b = 10 feet
Distance from fulcrum to point where force is applied = a = 20 feet
How much force (F) must be applied to lift the weight?

   a. 80
   b. 40
   c. 20
   d. 10

13. Which of the following is an example of torque?

   a. The wheel of a pulley turning
   b. A piston moving
   c. A horse pulling a load
   d. A tow truck pulling a vehicle

14. Which of the following floor plans match the house shown below?

a.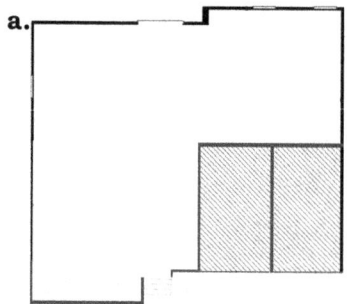

b.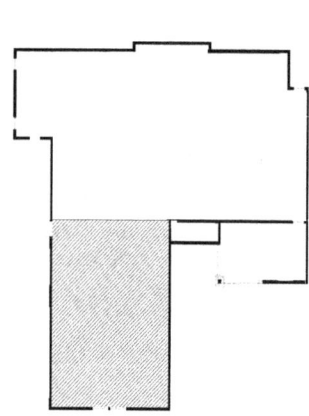

c.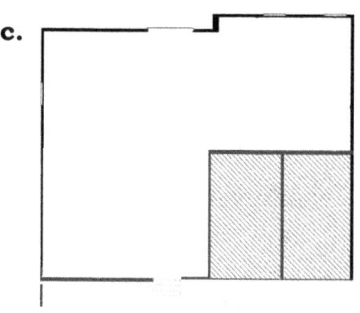

d.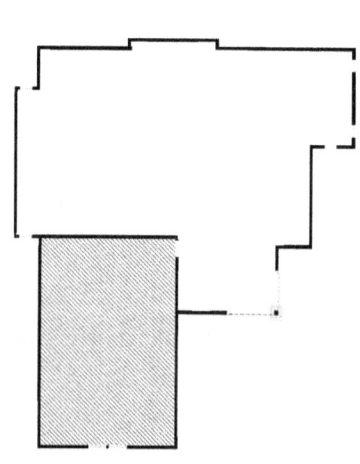

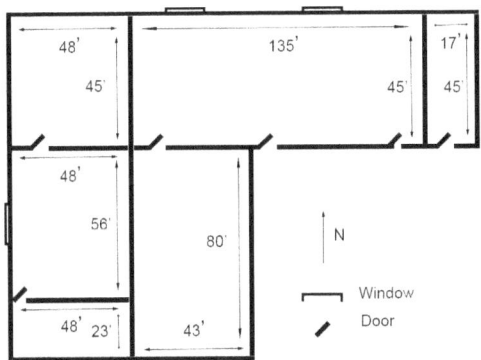

Note: figure not drawn to scale

15. What is the north south width of the house above?

   a. 124
   b. 100
   c. 200
   d. 224

16. What is the east west length of the house above?

   a. 200
   b. 124
   c. 100
   d. 224

17. Which of the following floor plans match the house shown below?

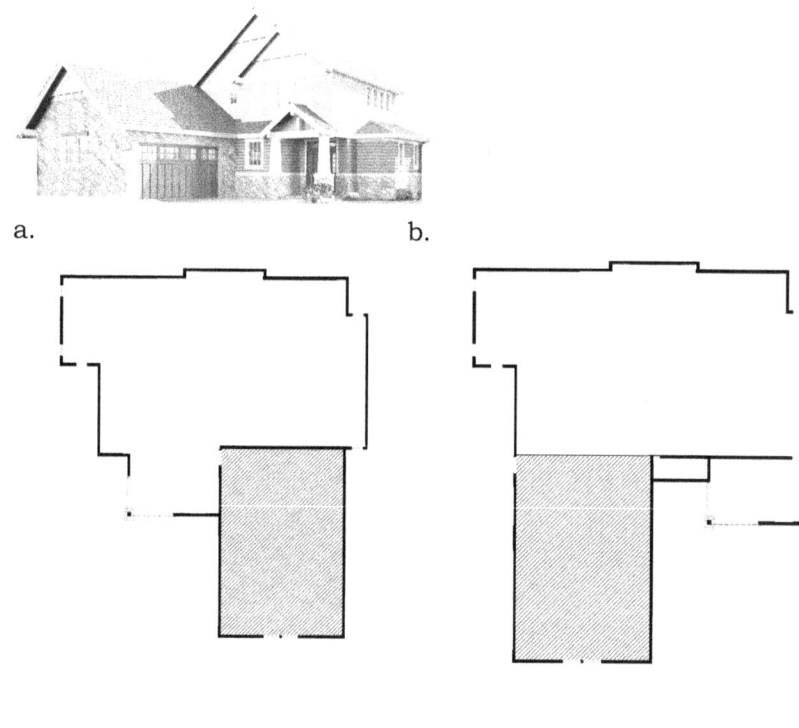

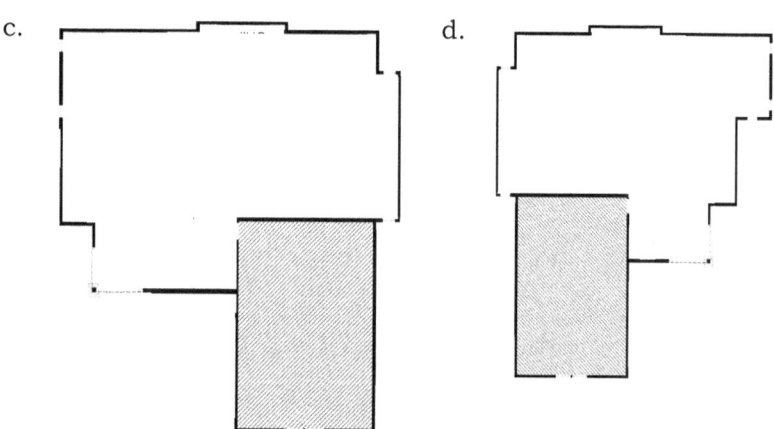

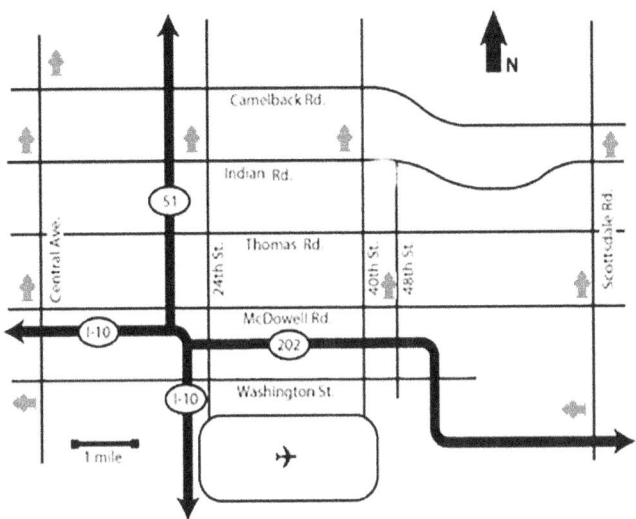

18. Consider the map above. How many hydrants are on Indian Road?

    a. 1
    b. 2
    c. 3
    d. 4

19. What is the best route from the east exit of the airport to the corner of Camelback and Central?

a. Exit the airport onto 40th st. and proceed north, turn left on Camelback Rd. and proceed straight to the corner of Central Ave.

b. Exit the airport on 24th st. and proceed north, turn left on Camelback Rd. and proceed straight to the corner of Central Ave.

c. Exit the airport onto 40th st. and turn west on hwy 202, then north on hwy 1-10, then right on hwy 51 then exit on Camelback Rd. and proceed strait to the corner of central.

d. None of the above.

20. About how far is the corner of Scottsdale Rd. and Thomas Rd. to the corder of Central Ave. and Thomas Rd.?

a. 4 miles

b. 3 miles

c. 5 miles

d. 7 miles

Mapping

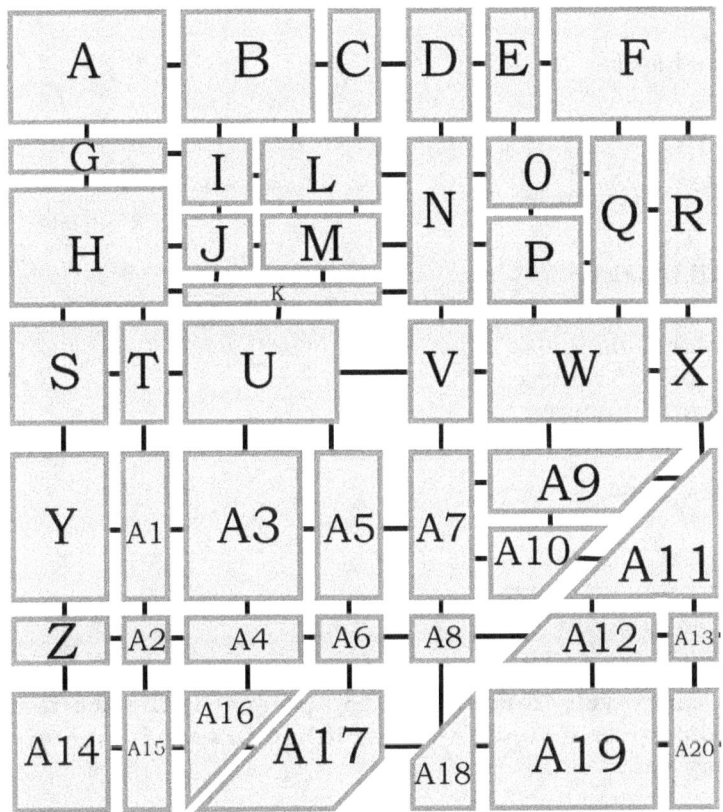

Map Key

Each Square labeled A to Z and A1 to A20 represent the corner of an intersection. The lines between the squares represent a city block. The intersections and city blocks fall into 3 categories.

Large blocks: A, B,F, H, N, Q, R, U, W, Y, A3, A5, A7, A9, A11, A14, A17, A19
Small blocks: C, D, E, I. J, L, M, O, P, S, T, V, X, A1, A4, A10, Z, A12, A15, A16, A18, A20

Mini blocks: G, K, A2, A6, A8, A13

The time it to travel between city block is:

Large blocks

In a car: 4 minutes
On a bike: 6 minutes
On foot: 10 minutes

Small Blocks

In a car: 3 minutes
On a bike: 5 minutes
On foot: 8 minutes

Mini Blocks

In a car: 2 minutes
On a bike: 4 minutes
On foot: 6 minutes

1. A car travels from block X to A6. What is the shortest possible time it would spend if it had to spend 2 minutes to buy gas?

    a. 15 minutes

    b. 12 minutes

    c. 17 minutes

    d. 14 minutes

2. How fast can you walk from block B to V without passing through blocks L and N?

    a. 52 minutes

    b. 42 minutes

    c. 45 minutes

    d. 38 minutes

3. A pizza delivery boy on bike in block A9 has to make a delivery in A20. What is the shortest time it would take him to get if he rides his bike the first 2 blocks and walks the rest of the way?

   a. 18 minutes
   b. 20 minutes
   c. 17 minutes
   d. 22 minutes

4. A car moves from block Y to block A17. Along the way it goes through block A2 and A5. What is the shortest time it could have taken if it is not allowed to go through the same block twice?

   a. 19 minutes
   b. 29 minutes
   c. 20 minutes
   d. 22 minutes

5. What is the shortest time it would take to bike from block H to block A4 if you must pass through block Y?

   a. 30 minutes
   b. 26 minutes
   c. 18 minutes
   d. 28 minutes

6. How fast can it take a police car to travel from block Z to V if it has to spend 15 seconds extra at each intersection it drives pass?

   a. 15 minutes 45 seconds
   b. 16 minutes 45 seconds
   c. 17 minutes
   d. 17 minutes 45 seconds

7. Which of the following would be the shortest?

Driving from block Z to A12
Walking from block A to D
Driving from A to C and then walking to D
Riding a bike from block T to A14

    a. driving from block z to a12
    b. walking from block a to d
    c. driving from a to c and then walking to d
    d. riding a bike from block t to a14

8. Which of these would take the most time?

Walking from A3 to K
Riding a bike from A3 to A10
Driving a car from A3 to S
Riding a bike from A3 to y, then driving a car to H

    a. walking from a3 to k

    b. riding a bike from a3 to a10

    c. driving a car from a3 to s

    d. riding a bike from a3 to y, then driving a car to h

9. If you had to spend 15 extra seconds at each intersection, how long would it take from block F to block V by bike, using the shortest route?

    a. 15 minutes

    b. 12 minutes

    c. 14 minutes

    d. 17 minutes

10. A driver needs to go from block F to V. How many possible route combinations can he use if he must pass through only 4 blocks between F and V?

    a. 5 routes
    b. 4 routes
    c. 3 routes
    d. 6 routes

11. A driver needs to drive from block F to V. What is the fastest time he can use if he must pass through only 4 blocks between F and V?

    a. 15 minutes
    b. 16 minutes
    c. 17 minutes
    d. 19 minutes

12. How fast would a bike rider move from block H to X?

    a. 24 minutes
    b. 27 minutes
    c. 25 minutes
    d. 26 minutes

13. How long would it take a man to move from block H to X if he drove a car the first 3 blocks and then rode a bike the rest of the way, using the fastest route?

    a. 18 minutes
    b. 21 minutes
    c. 22 minutes
    d. 20 minutes

14. How long would it take to move from block D to A6, by car for the first block, by bike for the next 2 blocks and then on foot the rest of the way, using the fastest route?

a. 30 minutes
b. 25 minutes
c. 32 minutes
d. 28 minutes

15. How fast does it take by bike from block G to P with a one minute stop at each intersection?

a. 22 minutes
b. 19 minutes
c. 23 minutes
d. 25 minutes

Situation Judgment

Scenario 1

You have the knowledge that company property has been going missing for some time now. You noticed a colleague putting small things from the office in her handbag several times and suspect she is responsible.

What should you do?

a. Find ways to get more evidence or catch her in the act.

b. Face your colleague and ask her about what you have noticed then inform your manager of your suspicion.

c. Raise the issue in a meeting and mention that you suspect your colleague.

d. Don't do anything. Your colleague will be caught if she is guilty.

Scenario 2

You walk into the washroom and find a colleague crying. What should you do?

    a. Walk out and give them peace.

    b. Find the manager and leave the situation to them.

    c. Ask whether they are fine and if there is anything you can do to help.

    d. Give them a hug at tell them everything will be okay.

Scenario 3

You have been working with a company for more than three years. During this period, you have familiarized yourself with all polices governing the company's operations. On this particular day, your immediate supervisor asks you to undertake a task which definitely goes against company policies.

What should you do?

    a. Do as the supervisor asks and disregard the company policies

    b. Decline to do what the supervisor asks of you.

    c. Explain to the supervisor that the action goes against the policies

    d. Ask the supervisor whether he knows the policies of the company

Scenario 4

You are working on a task that calls for skills that you don't have. You need help from your work mates who have the required skills.

How would you go about seeking collaboration?

    a. Make a thorough analysis of all the parameters at play and act decisively.

    b. Ask for collaboration from other team members.

    c. Act immediately without thinking.

    d. Fail to take any action.

Scenario 5

Conflict in the workplace is common in most organizations. Your co-worker falsely accuses you and you feel resentment towards him. The two of you get into an extended conflict and antagonistic relationship, which could see production affected.

How should you handle this situation?

    a. Apologize to your coworker.

    b. Have a supervisor involved in resolving the conflict.

    c. Act normal and pretend that nothing wrong will happen.

    d. Ask for an apology from your friend.

Scenario 6

You are on shift and performing your normal duties, when something very urgent comes up. The issue is extremely demanding and none of your colleagues have handled this type of situation before.

How should you handle this situation?

    a. Make a thorough analysis of all the parameters at play and act decisively.

    b. Ask for collaboration from other team members on the appropriate course of action.

    c. Act immediately without thinking

    d. Fail to take any action

Scenario 7

It's a bright Monday morning and you show up to work as usual. Before you get to the main door, you over-hear your team members shouting and yelling at each other. It seems like a really big fight is going on. It's obvious that your coworkers disagree on some very basic principles.

How should you go about bringing cohesion to your team?

    a. Refer this matter to your supervisor

    b. Ask what could be wrong and offer advice

    c. Talk to each of the employees separately

    d. Discuss this with the entire team and ask for solutions

Scenario 8

You have a customer that is very happy with your services and wants you to work in their hotel.

What should you do?

    a. Tell the customer you are pleased that he is happy but you are happy with your current place of work

    b. Tell the customer you will be happy to take the job immediately

    c. Tell the customer that proposal is inappropriate and you will not respond

    d. Tell the customer that you will inform the manager they are looking for some extra staff

Scenario 9

During a fire incident, you notice that one of your team members is not responding to radio calls. What should you do?

    a. Ignore it and continue with your task.

    b. Report the issue to the team leader immediately.

    c. Try to contact the team member through other means.

    d. Assume they are busy and wait for them to respond.

Scenario 10

You are leading a team during a rescue operation, and one of your team members suggests an alternative approach. How should you respond?

    a. Dismiss their suggestion and stick to your plan.

    b. Listen to their suggestion and consider its merits.

    c. Ignore the suggestion and continue with your plan.

    d. Criticize them for questioning your leadership.

Scenario 11

During a training exercise, you notice that a new team member is struggling with a task. What should you do?

    a. Ignore them and focus on your own performance.

    b. Offer assistance and guidance to help them improve.

    c. Report their struggle to the supervisor.

    d. Criticize them for their lack of skill.

Scenario 12

In the middle of a high-pressure situation, a team member makes a mistake. How should you handle it?

    a. Publicly reprimand them to set an example.

    b. Address the mistake calmly and provide constructive feedback.

    c. Ignore the mistake and hope it doesn't happen again.

    d. Blame them for the mistake and move on.

Scenario 13

You are coordinating with another team during a large-scale emergency. How can you ensure effective communication?

    a. Use clear and concise language over the radio.

    b. Assume the other team understands your instructions.

    c. Only communicate when absolutely necessary.

    d. Rely on non-verbal signals.

Scenario 14

During a team meeting, a colleague interrupts you while you are speaking. How should you handle the situation?

    a. Interrupt them back to make your point.

    b. Politely ask them to let you finish before they speak.

    c. Ignore the interruption and continue speaking.

    d. Leave the meeting in frustration.

Scenario 15

You notice that a team member is consistently left out of group discussions. What should you do?

    a. Ignore it and focus on your own work.

    b. Encourage the team member to share their thoughts.

    c. Speak on their behalf during discussions.

    d. Avoid involving them in future discussions.

Answer Key

Reading Comprehension

1. A
The first paragraph provides a summary of firefighter's job. The second paragraph is mainly about different tasks a firefighter performs. The third paragraph is about being on-call. The fourth paragraph is about different types of fires. And the last paragraph is about forest firefighters.

2. C
Smoke jumpers are forest firefighters. The last paragraph highlights this fact.

3. D
All of the above. Choices A, B and C are all aims of the passage hence choice D is the correct response.

    a. to show that fire fighters work throughout the year
    b. outlines the work of fire fighters
    c. highlight the different types of firefighters

4. C
Firefighters most frequently respond to medical emergencies. This is clearly highlighted in the first paragraph.

5. A
Low blood sugar occurs both in diabetics and healthy adults.

6. B
None of the statements are the author's opinion.

7. A
The author's purpose is to inform.

8. A
The only statement that is **not** a detail is, "A doctor can diagnosis this medical condition by asking the patient questions and testing."

9. C

This question tests the reader's summarization skills. The use of the word "actually" in describing what kind of people poets are, as well as other moments like this, may lead readers to selecting choice B or D, but the author is more information than trying to persuade readers. The author gives no indication that she loves poetry (B) or that people, students specifically (D), should write poems. Choice A is incorrect because the style and content of this paragraph do not match those of a foreword; forewords usually focus on the history or ideas of a specific poem to introduce it more fully and help it stand out against other poems. The author here focuses on several poems and gives broad statements. Instead, she tells a kind of story about poems, giving three very broad time periods in which to discuss them, thereby giving a brief history of poetry, as choice C states.

10. A

This question tests the reader's summarization skills. Key words in the topic sentences of each of the paragraphs ("oldest," "Renaissance," "modern") should give the reader an idea that the author is moving chronologically. The opening and closing sentence-paragraphs are broad and talk generally. Choice B seems reasonable, but epic poems are mentioned in two paragraphs, eliminating the idea that only new types of poems are used in each paragraph. Choice C is also easily eliminated because the author clearly mentions several different poets, groups of people, and poems. Choice D also seems reasonable, considering that the author does move from older forms of poetry to newer forms, but use of "so (that)" makes this statement false, for the author gives no indication that she is rushing (the paragraphs are about the same size) or that she prefers modern poetry.

11. D

This question tests the reader's attention to detail. The key word is "invented"--it ties together the Mesopotamians, who invented the written word, and the fact that they, as the inventors, also invented and used poetry. The other selections focus on other details mentioned in the passage, such as that the Renaissance's admiration of the Greeks (C) and that Beowulf is in Old English (A). Choice B may seem like an attractive answer because it is unlike the others and because the idea of heroes seems rooted in ancient and early civilizations.

12. B
This question tests the reader's vocabulary and contextualization skills. "Telling" is not an unusual word, but it may be used here in a way that is not familiar to readers, as an adjective rather than a verb in gerund form. Choice A may seem like the obvious answer to a reader looking for a verb to match the use they are familiar with. If the reader understands that the word is being used as an adjective and that choice A is a ploy, they may opt to select choice D, "wordy," but it does not make sense in context. Choice C can be easily eliminated, and doesn't have any connection to the paragraph or passage. "Significant" (B) does make sense contextually, especially relative to the phrase "give insight" used later in the sentence.

13. C
This question tests the reader's vocabulary skills. The uses of the negatives "but" and "less," especially right next to each other, may confuse readers into answering with choices A or D, which list words that are the opposite of "militant." Readers may also be confused by the comparison of healthy people with what is being described as an overly healthy person -- both people are good, but the reader may look for which one is "worse" in the comparison, and therefore stray toward the opposite words.

One key to understanding the meaning of "militant" is to look at the root; and then easily associate it with "military" and gain a sense of what the word signifies: defense (especially considered that the immune system defends the body). Choice C is correct over B because "militant" is an adjective, just as the words in C are, whereas the words in choice B are nouns.

14. C
This question tests the reader's understanding of function within writing. The other choices are all details included surrounding the quoted text, and may therefore confuse the reader. Choice A somewhat contradicts what is said earlier in the paragraph, which is that tests and treatments are improving, and probably doctors are along with them, but the paragraph doesn't actually mention doctors, and the subject of the question is the medicine. Choice B may seem correct

to readers who aren't careful to understand that, while the author does mention the large number of people effected, the author is touching on the realities of living with allergies, rather than the likelihood of curing all allergies. Similarly, while the author does mention the "balance" of the body, which is easily associated with "wholesome," the author is not really making an argument and especially is not making an extreme statement that allergy medicines should be outlawed. Again, because the article's tone is on living with allergies, choice C is an appropriate choice that fits with the title and content of the text.

15. B

This question tests the reader's inference skills. The text does not state who is doing the recommending, but the use of the "patients," as well as the general context of the passage, lends itself to the logical partner, "doctors," choice B.

The author does mention the recommendation but doesn't present it as her own (i.e. "I recommend that"), so choice A may be eliminated. It may seem plausible that people with allergies (choice D) may recommend medicines or products to other people with allergies, but the text does not necessarily support this interaction taking place. Choice C may be selected because the EpiPen is specifically mentioned, but the use of the phrase "such as" when it is introduced is not limiting enough to assume the recommendation is coming from its creators.

16. B

This question tests the reader's summarization skills. Choice A is a very broad statement that may or may not be true, and seems to be in context, but has nothing to do with the passage. The author does mention that the statue was probably used on a temple dedicated to the Greek gods (D), but in no way discusses or argues for the gods' attitude toward or claim on these temples or its faucets. Nike does indeed lead the gods into a war (the Titan war), as choice C suggests, but this is not mentioned by the passage and students who know this may be drawn to this answer but have not done a close enough analysis of the text that is actually in the passage. Choice B is appropriately expository, and connects the titular emphasis to the idea that the Greek gods are very important to Greek culture.

17. C

This question tests the reader's summarization skills. The test for question choice C is pulled straight from the paragraph, but is not word-for-word, so it may seem too obvious to be the right answer. The passage does talk about Nike being the goddess of war, as choice A states, but the third paragraph only touches on it and it is an inference that soldiers destroyed the statue, when this question is asking specifically for what the third paragraph actually stated. Choice B is also straight from the text, with a minor but key change: the inclusion of the words "all" and "never" are too limiting and the passage does not suggest that these limits exist. If a reader selects choice D, they are also making an inference that is misguided for this type of question. The paragraph does state that the arms and head are "lost" but does not suggest who lost them.

18. A

This question tests the reader's ability to recognize function in writing. Choice B can be eliminated based on the purpose of the passage, which is expository and not persuasive. The author may or may not feel this way, but the passage does not show evidence of being argumentative for that purpose. Choices C and D are both details found in the text, but neither of them encompasses the entire message of the passage, which has an overall message of learning about culture from art and making guesses about how the two are related, as suggested by choice A.

19. D

This question tests the reader's ability to understand function within writing. Most of the possible selections are very general statements which may or may not be true. It probably is a student who is taking the test on which this question is featured (A), but the author makes no address to the test taker and is not talking to the audience in terms of the test. Likewise, it may also be true that students read more than adults (C), mandated by schools and grades, but the focus on the verb "read" in the first sentence is too narrow and misses the larger purpose of the passage; the same could be said for selection B. While all the statements could be true, choice D is the most germane, and infers the purpose of the passage without making assumptions that could be incorrect.

20. A
Sound is a new way to extinguish fires being studied.

21. C
The purpose is to provide information about fires.

22. C
Electrical fires cannot be extinguished by water. This can be inferred from the writers experience when he attempted to extinguish the fire in the garage.

23. D
This question tests the reader's summarization skills. The question is asking very generally about the message of the passage, and the title, "Ways Characters Communicate in Theater," is one indication of that. The other choices A, B, and C are all directly from the text, and therefore readers may be inclined to select one of them, but are too specific to encapsulate the entirety of the passage and its message.

24. B
The paragraph on soliloquies mentions "To be or not to be," and it is from the context of that paragraph that readers may understand that because "To be or not to be" is a soliloquy, Hamlet will be introspective, or thoughtful, while delivering it. It is true that actors deliver soliloquies alone, and may be "solitary" (A), but "thoughtful" (B) is more true to the overall idea of the paragraph. Readers may choose C because drama and theater can be used interchangeably and the passage mentions that soliloquies are unique to theater (and therefore drama), but this answer is not specific enough to the paragraph in question. Readers may pick up on the theme of life and death and Hamlet's true intentions and select that he is "hopeless" (D), but those themes are not discussed either by this paragraph or passage, as a close textual reading and analysis confirms.

25. C
This question tests the reader's grammatical skills. Choice B seems logical, but parenthesis are actually considered to be a stronger break in a sentence than commas are, and along this line of thinking, actually disrupt the sentence more. Choices A and D make comparisons between theater and film that are simply not made in the passage, and may or may not be true. This detail does clarify the statement that asides are most unique to theater by adding that it is not completely unique to theater, which may have been why the author didn't chose not to delete it and instead used parentheses to designate the detail's importance (C).

26. C
This question tests the reader's vocabulary and contextualization skills. Choice A may or may not be true, but focuses on the wrong function of the word "give" and ignores the rest of the sentence, which is more relevant to what the passage is discussing. Choices B and D may also be selected if the reader depends too literally on the word "give," failing to grasp the more abstract function of the word that is the focus of choice C, which also properly acknowledges the entirety of the passage and its meaning.

27. A
According to the gauge, the limit of the safe working range is about 80 PSI.

28. A
The Save the Children's fund has raised $12,000 out of $20,000, or 12/20. Simplifying, 12/20 = 3/5

29. D
Fires are compared to hurricanes as they are both unpredictable. This is clearly stated in the first paragraph.

30. B
Overconfidence can cause complacency. Choices A and C may seem plausible if you are in a hurry and don't check the passage carefully. However choice B is correct.

Listening Comprehension

1. B

Fire extinguishers are typically used for small fires and not intended for out-of-control fires, such as one which has reached the ceiling, or endangers the user.

2. C

Fire extinguishers are typically inspected every year, although some jurisdictions require more frequent inspections.

3. A

The two most common types of fire extinguishers are stored pressure and cartridge-operated.

4. A

Hand-held fire extinguishers weigh between 1 and 30 pounds.

5. C

The burning of organic matter like wood, or the incomplete combustion of gas, incandescent solid particles called soot produce the familiar red-orange glow of 'fire.'

6. B

Complete combustion of gas has a dim blue color.

7. A

Usually oxygen is necessary for a fire to burn.

8. D

There is no flame in combustion engines.

9. C

One of the positive effects of fire is returning nutrients to the soil.

10. A

A positive effect on the eco-system is rejuvenating the soil.

11. C

A negative effect of fire is air pollution.

12. C
From the passage, "some adult insects live underwater and are excellent swimmers."

13. D
From the passage, "Many insects communicate with sound."

14. C
Insects are mostly solitary, but some are social like ants and bees.

15. A
Choice A is a re-wording of text from the passage.

16. D
This question is designed to confuse by presenting different options for the 2 chemicals, oxygen and carbon dioxide. One is produced and one is reduced.

17. A
The three main emergency services are fire departments, emergency medical and police.

18. B
The three goals of the fire department are to save lives, protect property and protect the environment.

19. B
Dalmatians are traditionally associated with fire fighters.

20. B
From the Passage, "Fire departments only used dogs for rescue operations, and keep them away from fires. "

Mathematics

1. A
1/3 X 3/4 = 3/12 = 1/4

2. D
75/1500 = 15/300 = 3/60 = 1/20

3. D
3.14 + 2.73 = 5.87 and 5.87 + 23.7 = 29.57

4. B
Spent 15% - 100% - 15% = 85%

5. C
To convert a decimal to a fraction, take the places of decimal as your denominator, here 2, so in 0.27, '7' is in the 100th place, so the fraction is 27/100 and 0.33 becomes 33/100.

Next estimate the answer quickly to eliminate obvious wrong choices. 27/100 is about 1/4 and 33/100 is 1/3. 1/3 is slightly larger than 1/4, and 1/4 + 1/4 is 1/2, so the answer will be slightly larger than 1/2.

Looking at the choices, Choice A can be eliminated since 3/6 = 1/2. Choice D, 2/7 is less than 1/2 and can be eliminated. So the answer is going to be Choice B or Choice C.

Do the calculation, 0.27 + 0.33 = 0.60 and 0.60 = 60/100 = 3/5, Choice C is correct.

6. D
3.13 + 7.87 = 11 and 11 X 5 = 55

7. B
2/4 X 3/4 = 6/16, and reduced to the lowest terms = 3/8

8. D
2/3 - 2/5 = 10-6 /15 = 4/15

9. C
2/7 + 2/3 = 6+14 /21 (21 is the common denominator) = 20/21

10. B
2/3 x 60 = 40 and 1.5 x 75 = 15, 40 + 15 = 55

11. C
This is an easy question, and shows how you can solve some questions without doing the calculations. The question is, 8 is what percent of 40. Take easy percentages for an approximate answer and see what you get.

10% is easy to calculate because you can drop the zero, or move the decimal point. 10% of 40 = 4, and 8 = 2 X 4, so, 8 must be 2 X 10% = 20%.

Here are the calculations which confirm the quick approximation.
8/40 = X/100 = 8 * 100 / 40X = 800/40 = X = 20

12. D
This is the same type of question which illustrates another method to solve quickly without doing the calculations. The question is, 9 is what percent of 36?

Ask, what is the relationship between 9 and 36? 9 X 4 = 36 so they are related by a factor of 4. If 9 is related to 36 by a factor of 4, then what is related to 100 (to get a percent) by a factor of 4?

To visualize:

9 X 4 = 36
Z X 4 = 100

So the answer is 25. 9 has the same relation to 36 as 25 has to 100.
Here are the calculations which confirm the quick approximation.
9/36 = X/100 = 9 * 100 / 36X = 900/36 = 25

13. C
3/10 * 90 = 3 * 90/10 = 27

14. A
.4/100 * 36 = .4 * 36/100 = .144

15. A
1000g = 1kg., 0.007 = 1000 x 0.007 = 7g.

16. C
4 quarts = 1 gallon, 16 quarts = 16/4 = 4 gallons

17. D
1,000 meters = 1 kilometer, 200 m = 200/1,000 = 0.2 km.

18. B
12 inches = 1 ft., 72 inches = 72/12 = 6 feet

19. C
1 yard = 3 feet, 3 yards = 3 feet x 3 = 9 feet

20. B
0.45 kg = 1 pound, 1 kg. = 1/0.45 and 45 kg = 1/0.45 x 45 = 99.208, or 100 pounds

21. C
1 g = 1,000 mg. 0.63 g = 0.63 x 1,000 = 630 mg.

22. D
The price increased by $5 ($25-$20). The percent increase is 5/20 x 100 = 5 x 5=25%

23. C
The price decreased by $5 ($25-$20). The percent increase = 5/25 x 100 = 5 x 4 =20%

24. D
30/100 x 150 = 3 x 15 = 45 (increase in number of correct answers). So the number of correct answers on the second test = 150 + 45 = 195

25. B
Let total number of players= X
Let the number of players with long hair = Y and the number of players with short hair = Z
Then X = 4 + Z
Y = 12% of X
Z = X - 4
12.5% of X = 4
Converting from decimal to fraction gives 12.5% = 125/10 x 1/100 = 125/1000, therefore 12.5% of = 125/1000X = 4
Solve for X by multiplying both sides by 1000/125, X = 4 x 1000/125 = 32
Z = x – 4
Z = 32 – 4
z or number of short haired players = 28

26. D
2 glasses are broken for 43 customers so 1 glass breaks for every 43/2 customers served, therefore 10 glasses implies 43/2 x 10 = 215

27. D
As the lawn is square, the length of one side will be the square root of the area. $\sqrt{62,500}$ = 250 meters. So, the perimeter is 4 times the length of one side:

250 * 4 = 1000 meters.

Since each meter costs $5.5, the total cost of the fence will be 1000 * 5.5 = $5,500.

28. D
The price of all the single items is same and there are 13 total items. So the total cost will be 13 × 1.3 = $16.9. After 3.5 percent tax this amount will become 16.9 × 1.035 = $17.5.

29. B
The distribution is at three different rates and amounts:

$6.4 per 20 kilograms to 15 shops ... 20 * 15 = 300 kilograms distributed

$3.4 per 10 kilograms to 12 shops ... 10 * 12 = 120 kilograms distributed

550 - (300 + 120) = 550 - 420 = 130 kilograms left. This amount is distributed by 5 kilogram portions. So, this means that there are 130/5 = 26 shops.

$1.8 per 130 kilograms.

We need to find the amount he earned overall these distributions.

$6.4 per 20 kilograms : 6.4 * 15 = $96 for 300 kilograms

$3.4 per 10 kilograms : 3.4 * 12 = $40.8 for 120 kilograms

$1.8 per 5 kilograms : 1.8 * 26 = $46.8 for 130 kilograms

So, he earned 96 + 40.8 + 46.8 = $ 183.6

The total cost of distribution is given as $10

The profit is found by: Money earned - money spent ... It is important to remember that he bought 550 kilograms of potatoes for $165 at the beginning:

Profit = 183.6 - 10 - 165 = $8.6

30. B
We check the fractions in the question. We see that there is a "half" (that is 1/2) and 3/7. So, we multiply the denominators of these fractions to decide how to name the total money. We say that Mr. Johnson has 14x at the beginning; he gives half of this, meaning 7x, to his family. $250 to his landlord. He has 3/7 of his money left. 3/7 of 14x is equal to:

14x * (3/7) = 6x

So,

Spent money is: 7x + 250

Unspent money is: 6x

Total money is: 14x

We write an equation: total money = spent money + unspent money

14x = 7x + 250 + 6x

14x - 7x - 6x = 250

x = 250

We are asked to find the total money that is 14x:

14x = 14 * 250 = $3500

Mechanical Aptitude

1. A
Mechanical advantage is the ratio of energy input to energy output, typically where the input is less than the output. Mechanical advantage is a measure of the force amplification achieved by using a tool, mechanical device or machine system. Ideally, the device preserves the input power and simply trades off forces against movement to obtain a desired amplification in the output force. The model for this is the law of the lever. Machine components designed to manage forces and movement in this way are called mechanisms. [11]

2. B
The ratio of mechanical advantage of a simple pulley is 1:1.

3. A
The farther away from the fulcrum, the faster the object will move.

4. B
Examples of wedges include the cutting edge of scissors, knives, screwdrivers, doorstops, nails axes and chisels.

5. B
The greater the distance over which the force is applied, the smaller the force required (to lift the load).

6. C
Call the input gear G_1 and the output gear G_2. Call the speed of G_1, S_1 and the number of teeth T_1. Similarly for G_2, we have S_2 and T_2.

Given data:
$S_1 = 100$
$T_1 = 30$
$S_2 = $ unknown
$T_2 = 40$

We know that $S_1 \times T_1 = S_2 \times T_2$
So, $100 \times 30 = S_2 \times 40$
$S_2 = 3000/40 = 75$ rpm

7. B
Call the input gear G_1 and the output gear G_2. Call the speed of G_1, S_1 and the number of teeth T_1. Similarly for G_2, we have S_2 and T_2.

Given data
$S_1 = 50$
$T_1 = 100$
$S_2 =$ unknown
$T_2 = 20$

We know that $S_1 \times T_1 = S_2 \times T_2$

So, $50 \times 100 = S_2 \times 20$
$S_2 = 5000/20 = 250$ rpm

8. B
Notice the weight is attached to one end of the rope and to one pulley. The force required to lift a 100 pound weight with this arrangement is $100/3 = 33$.

9. A
A Robertson screwdriver would be used.

10. C
50 pounds of force much be exerted downward on the rope to lift the 200 pound weight. Since there are 4 pulleys, each will take 1/4 of the load. $200/4 = 50$ pounds.

11. B
Up-and-down or back-and-forth motion is called reciprocal motion.

12. B
To solve for F, Weight X b (distance from fulcrum to weight) = Force X a (distance from fulcrum to point where force is applied)
$80 \times 10 = F \times 20$
$800/20 = F$
$F = 40$

13. A
The wheel of a pulley turning is an example of torque. Torque, moment or moment of force, is the tendency of a force to rotate an object about an axis, fulcrum, or pivot. Just as a force is a push or a pull, a torque can be thought of as a twist to an object. [12]

14. A
Choice B shows the garage on the wrong side. Choice does not show the bay window. Choice D does not show the second dormer.

15. A
The north-south width of the house pictured is 124 ft.

16. A
The east-west length of the house is 200 ft.

17. D
Choice A has the porch and the garage on the wrong side. The porch and side bay window on the right hand corner are incorrect. Choice C has the garage on the wrong side and the left hand side profile incorrect. Choice D has the front porch incorrect.

18. D
There are 4 hydrants on Indian Rd.

19. A
Choice A is the most direct route with the fewest turns. Choice B exits from the west airport exit, not the east. Choice C involves more turns and a number of short turns and exits from highways. Choice A is the best answer.

20. C
It is about 5 miles from the corner of Scottsdale Rd. and Thomas Rd. to the corder of Central Ave. and Thomas Rd.

Mapping

1. D
The fastest route is through blocks X – A11 – A12 – A8 – A6. Time by car is 12 plus 2 minutes to buy gas is 14 minutes.

2. B
The fastest route is B – I – J – K – U – V. Time on foot is 42 minutes.

3. A
The Fastest route is A9 – A11 – A13 – A20. By bike the first two blocks would take 12 minutes. To walk the last block would take 6 minutes. Total time is 18 minutes.

4. D
Fastest route is Y – Z – A2 – A1 – A3 – A5 – A6 – A7. By car it would take 22 minutes.

5. B
Fastest route is H – S – Y – Z – A2 – A4. Time by bike is 26 minutes.
6. B
The fastest route from Z to V is Z – A2- A4 – A6 – A8 – A7 – V. Total drive time is 16 minutes. From Z would go through 5 intersections. 15 seconds at each intersection is 45 seconds. Total time is 16 minutes, 45 seconds.

7. A
Driving from block Z to A12 would take 12 minutes.
Walking from block A to D would take 28 minutes
Driving from A to C and then walking to D would take 16 minutes
Riding a bike from block T to A14 would take 19 minutes.
The shortest trip would be driving from block Z to A12.

8. A
Walking from A3 to K would take 20 minutes
Riding a bike from A3 to A10 would take 11 minutes
Driving a car from A3 to S would take 11 minutes
Riding a bike from A3 to y, then driving a car to H would take 17 minutes
The most time would be to walk from A3 to K (A)

9. C
The shortest route from F to V is F – Q – W – V. The time on bike is 14 minutes.

10. A
Possible routes between F and V that goes through just 4 blocks are?
F – Q – R – X – W – V
F – E – O – P - W – V
F - E - O - Q - W – V
F - Q - W - P -N – V
F - Q - O - P - W – V
There are 5 possible routes.

11. C
There are 5 possible routes from block F to V that goes through just 4 blocks. 4 of the 5 routes take the least time of 17 minutes each.

12. B
The fastest route from H to X is H – K – N – V – W – X. On a bike that would take 27 minutes.

13. D
The fastest route from H to X is H – K – N – V – W – X. On foot for the first 3 blocks, it would take 9 minutes plus 11 minutes by bike to X. Total time is 20 minutes.

14. A
The fastest route is D – N – V – A7 – A8 - A6. To drive the first block is 3 minutes, then by bike the next 2 blocks is 11 minutes, and the on foot the last 2 blocks is 16 minutes. Total time is 30 minutes.

15. C
The fastest route is G – I – L – N – P. By bike it would take 20 minutes. Going through intersections I, L and N, is 3 minutes. Total time is 23 minutes.

Situation Judgment

1. B

This is the right thing to do as it will give you the chance to discuss the matter with your colleague first and clear ambiguity. It is also your responsibility to report the matter to your manager.

2. C

Response C is appropriate as shows that you have empathy. Even if you are not able to help the colleague will feel more relieved as a problem shared is a problem half solved.

3. C

It is possible the supervisor is unaware of a policy. It therefore becomes important to speak with them politely.

Rarely are supervisors wrong. However sometimes unexpected things happen, but that does not allow you to do something you know violates company policy (Choice A). Declining to do the task (Choice B) without explanation is not likely to be taken well by your superior. Generally supervisors know the policies better than you although it is possible (Choice D). Choice C is the better choice.

4. B

Two heads are better than one. By allowing others to have an input in the final decision, you not only reduce unnecessary resistance but also increase employee commitment. To be effective, a leader should ensure team members are part of the decision-making process. Being involved gives them a sense of importance and belonging.

It is possible to make a thorough analysis of the factors involved in this and assume that one is able to make a decision that will be accepted by all (Choice A) however getting buy-in from everyone is a better strategy. Choices C and D are Obviously wrong choices and can be eliminated right away.

5. B

Involving a neutral person (the supervisor) in conflict resolution leads to better understanding amongst the discontented parties. By involving a third party, you can diffuse the situation quickly and amicably. The leader offers proper guidance and issues directions to safeguard the interests of the organization.

It is not a sure thing that issuing an apology would bring to an end of the conflict (choice A) – more than that is required. Similarly choice C, is not a solution, as it may be taken as an accusation.

6. B
The phrase, two heads are better than one is a full of psychological truth. Asking for collaboration from others gives you a better chance to analyze the situation and decide wisely. It also makes them feel valued which raises their commitment levels.

This is a good choice but choice B, asking for collaboration is better. Choices C and D, taking action without information, is dangerous to the business. It is similar to driving a car blindfolded. It is hard to make the right call when faced with a new challenge. Making decisions under pressure is a challenge to most leaders. Chances of error are so high that consulting is not an choice, but a necessity.

7. A
Work-related conflict should be resolved by higher authority. An independent supervisor can provide the appropriate direction.

Choice D, discussing as a team and asking for solutions could deteriorate with members taking sides. Involve only the right people while solving such specific problems. Choice C, talking to each separately, may resolve but you are taking a chance you will not be able to resolve. Bringing it to you superiors is the best choice (choice A). Choice B, offering unsolicited advice would not be appreciated or resolve the situation.

8. A
This response is both polite and professional and shows your loyalty.

9. B

Communication is crucial in fire fighting. If a team member is not responding, it could indicate a serious problem. Reporting it to the team leader ensures that the issue is addressed promptly and safely.

10. B

Effective teamwork involves valuing each team member's input. Listening to suggestions can lead to better strategies and fosters a collaborative environment.

11. B

Teamwork involves supporting each other. Helping a struggling team member improves overall team performance and builds trust.

12. B

Constructive feedback helps team members learn from their mistakes without damaging morale. It's important to maintain a calm and supportive atmosphere.

13. A

Clear and concise communication is essential in emergency situations to avoid misunderstandings and ensure coordinated efforts.

14. B

Effective communication involves respecting each other's turn to speak. Politely asking to finish ensures that everyone has a chance to contribute without conflict.

15. B

Being a team player means ensuring that all members feel included and valued. Encouraging participation helps build a more cohesive and collaborative team.

Practice Test Questions Set 2

The practice test portion presents questions that are representative of the type of question you should expect to find on the GLEDHILL SHAW EXAM.

The questions here are for skill practice only.

For the best results, take this practice test as if it were the real exam. Set aside time when you will not be disturbed, and a location that is quiet and free of distractions. Read the instructions carefully, read each question carefully, and answer to the best of your ability.

Use the bubbles provided. When you have completed the Practice Test, check your answer against the Answer Key and read the explanation provided.

Reading Comprehension

	A	B	C	D	E		A	B	C	D	E
1	○	○	○	○	○	21	○	○	○	○	○
2	○	○	○	○	○	22	○	○	○	○	○
3	○	○	○	○	○	23	○	○	○	○	○
4	○	○	○	○	○	24	○	○	○	○	○
5	○	○	○	○	○	25	○	○	○	○	○
6	○	○	○	○	○	26	○	○	○	○	○
7	○	○	○	○	○	27	○	○	○	○	○
8	○	○	○	○	○	28	○	○	○	○	○
9	○	○	○	○	○	29	○	○	○	○	○
10	○	○	○	○	○	30	○	○	○	○	○
11	○	○	○	○	○						
12	○	○	○	○	○						
13	○	○	○	○	○						
14	○	○	○	○	○						
15	○	○	○	○	○						
16	○	○	○	○	○						
17	○	○	○	○	○						
18	○	○	○	○	○						
19	○	○	○	○	○						
20	○	○	○	○	○						

Listening Comprehension

	A	B	C	D
1	○	○	○	○
2	○	○	○	○
3	○	○	○	○
4	○	○	○	○
5	○	○	○	○
6	○	○	○	○
7	○	○	○	○
8	○	○	○	○
9	○	○	○	○
10	○	○	○	○
11	○	○	○	○
12	○	○	○	○
13	○	○	○	○
14	○	○	○	○
15	○	○	○	○
16	○	○	○	○
17	○	○	○	○
18	○	○	○	○
19	○	○	○	○
20	○	○	○	○

Mathematics

	A	B	C	D	E		A	B	C	D	E
1	○	○	○	○	○	21	○	○	○	○	○
2	○	○	○	○	○	22	○	○	○	○	○
3	○	○	○	○	○	23	○	○	○	○	○
4	○	○	○	○	○	24	○	○	○	○	○
5	○	○	○	○	○	25	○	○	○	○	○
6	○	○	○	○	○	26	○	○	○	○	○
7	○	○	○	○	○	27	○	○	○	○	○
8	○	○	○	○	○	28	○	○	○	○	○
9	○	○	○	○	○	29	○	○	○	○	○
10	○	○	○	○	○	30	○	○	○	○	○
11	○	○	○	○	○						
12	○	○	○	○	○						
13	○	○	○	○	○						
14	○	○	○	○	○						
15	○	○	○	○	○						
16	○	○	○	○	○						
17	○	○	○	○	○						
18	○	○	○	○	○						
19	○	○	○	○	○						
20	○	○	○	○	○						

Practice Test Questions 2

Mechanical Aptitude

	A	B	C	D
1	○	○	○	○
2	○	○	○	○
3	○	○	○	○
4	○	○	○	○
5	○	○	○	○
6	○	○	○	○
7	○	○	○	○
8	○	○	○	○
9	○	○	○	○
10	○	○	○	○
11	○	○	○	○
12	○	○	○	○
13	○	○	○	○
14	○	○	○	○
15	○	○	○	○
16	○	○	○	○
17	○	○	○	○
18	○	○	○	○
19	○	○	○	○
20	○	○	○	○

Map Reading

	A	B	C	D
1	○	○	○	○
2	○	○	○	○
3	○	○	○	○
4	○	○	○	○
5	○	○	○	○
6	○	○	○	○
7	○	○	○	○
8	○	○	○	○
9	○	○	○	○
10	○	○	○	○
11	○	○	○	○
12	○	○	○	○
13	○	○	○	○
14	○	○	○	○
15	○	○	○	○

Practice Test Questions 2

Situation Judgment

	A	B	C	D
1	○	○	○	○
2	○	○	○	○
3	○	○	○	○
4	○	○	○	○
5	○	○	○	○
6	○	○	○	○
7	○	○	○	○
8	○	○	○	○
9	○	○	○	○
10	○	○	○	○
11	○	○	○	○
12	○	○	○	○
13	○	○	○	○
14	○	○	○	○
15	○	○	○	○

Reading Comprehension

Questions 1 - 4 refer to the following passage.

Passage 1 - The Crusades

In 1095 Pope Urban II proclaimed the First Crusade with the intent and stated goal to restore Christian access to holy places in and around Jerusalem. Over the next 200 years there were 6 major crusades and numerous minor crusades in the fight for control of the "Holy Land." Historians are divided on the real purpose of the Crusades, some believing that it was part of a purely defensive war against Islamic conquest; some see them as part of a long-running conflict at the frontiers of Europe; and others see them as confident, aggressive, papal-led expansion attempts by Western Christendom. The impact of the crusades was profound, and judgment of the Crusaders ranges from laudatory to highly critical. However, all agree that the Crusades and wars waged during those crusades were brutal and often bloody. Several hundred thousand Roman Catholic Christians joined the Crusades, they were Christians from all over Europe.

Europe at the time was under the Feudal System, so while the Crusaders made vows to the Church, they also were beholden to their Feudal Lords. This led to the Crusaders not only fighting the Saracen, the commonly used word for Muslim at the time, but also each other for power and economic gain in the Holy Land. This infighting between the Crusaders is why many historians hold the view that the Crusades were simply a front for Europe to invade the Holy Land for economic gain in the name of the Church. Another factor contributing to this theory is that while the army of crusaders marched towards Jerusalem they pillaged the land as they went. The church and feudal Lords vowing to return the land to its original beauty, and inhabitants, this rarely happened though, as the Lords often kept the land for themselves. A full 800 years after the Crusades, Pope John Paul II expressed his sorrow for the massacre of innocent people and the lasting damage that the Medieval church caused in that area of the World.

1. What is the tone of this article?

    a. Subjective

    b. Objective

    c. Persuasive

    d. None of the Above

2. What can all historians agree on concerning the Crusades?

    a. It achieved great things

    b. It stabilized the Holy Land

    c. It was bloody and brutal

    d. It helped defend Europe from the Byzantine Empire

3. What impact did the feudal system have on the Crusades

    a. It unified the Crusaders

    b. It helped gather volunteers

    c. It had no effect on the Crusades

    d. It led to infighting, causing more damage than good

4. What does Saracen mean?

    a. Muslim

    b. Christian

    c. Knight

    d. Holy Land

Questions 5 - 8 refer to the following passage.

ABC Electric Warranty

ABC Electric Company warrants that its products are free from defects in material and workmanship. Subject to the conditions and limitations set forth below, ABC Electric will, at its option, either repair or replace any part of its products that prove defective due to improper workmanship or materials.

This limited warranty does not cover any damage to the product from improper installation, accident, abuse, misuse, natural disaster, insufficient or excessive electrical supply, abnormal mechanical or environmental conditions, or any unauthorized disassembly, repair, or modification.

This limited warranty also does not apply to any product on which the original identification information has been altered, or removed, has not been handled or packaged correctly, or has been sold as second-hand.

This limited warranty covers only repair, replacement, refund or credit for defective ABC Electric products, as provided above.

5. I tried to repair my ABC Electric blender, but could not, so can I get it repaired under this warranty?

    a. Yes, the warranty still covers the blender

    b. No, the warranty does not cover the blender

    c. Uncertain. ABC Electric may or may not cover repairs under this warranty

6. My ABC Electric fan is not working. Will ABC Electric provide a new one or repair this one?

    a. ABC Electric will repair my fan

    b. ABC Electric will replace my fan

    c. ABC Electric could either replace or repair my fan can request either a replacement or a repair.

7. My stove was damaged in a flood. Does this warranty cover my stove?

    a. Yes, it is covered.

    b. No, it is not covered.

    c. It may or may not be covered.

    d. ABC Electric will decide if it is covered

8. Which of the following is an example of improper workmanship?

    a. Missing parts

    b. Defective parts

    c. Scratches on the front

    d. None of the above

Questions 9 – 12 refer to the following passage.

Passage 2 - Women and Advertising

Only in the last few generations have media messages been so widespread and so readily seen, heard, and read by so many people. Advertising is an important part of both selling and buying anything from soap to cereal to jeans. For whatever reason, more consumers are women than are men. Media message are subtle but powerful, and more attention has been paid lately to how these message affect women. Of all the products that women buy, makeup, clothes, and other stylistic or cosmetic products are among the most popular. This means that companies focus their advertising on women, promising them that their product will make her feel, look, or smell better than the next company's product will. This competition has resulted in advertising that is more and more ideal and less and less possible for everyday women. However, because women do look to these ideals and the products they represent as how they can potentially become, many women have developed unhealthy attitudes about themselves when they have failed to become those ideals.

In recent years, more companies have tried to change advertisements to be healthier for women. This includes featuring models of more sizes and addressing a huge outcry against unfair tools such as airbrushing and photo editing. There is debate about what the right balance between real and ideal is, because fashion is also considered art and some changes are made to purposefully elevate fashionable products and signify that they are creative, innovative, and the work of individual people. Artists want their freedom protected as much as women do, and advertising agencies are often caught in the middle.

Some claim that the companies who make these changes are not doing enough. Many people worry that there are still not enough models of different sizes and different ethnicities. Some people claim that companies use this healthier type of advertisement not for the good of women, but because they would like to sell products to the women who are looking for these kinds of messages. This is also a hard balance to find: companies need to make money, and women need to feel respected.

While the focus of this change has been on women, advertising can also affect men, and this change will hopefully be a lesson on media for all consumers.

9. The second paragraph states that advertising focuses on women

   a. to shape what the ideal should be

   b. because women buy makeup

   c. because women are easily persuaded

   d. because of the types of products that women buy

10. According to the passage, fashion artists and female consumers are at odds because

   a. there is a debate going on and disagreement drives people apart

   b. both of them are trying to protect their freedom to do something

   c. artists want to elevate their products above the reach of women

   d. women are creative, innovative, individual people

11. The author uses the phrase "for whatever reason" in this passage to

   a. keep the focus of the paragraph on media messages and not on the differences between men and women

   b. show that the reason for this is unimportant

   c. argue that it is stupid that more women are consumers than men

   d. show that he or she is tired of talking about why media messages are important

12. This passage suggests that

   a. advertising companies are still working on making their messages better

   b. all advertising companies seek to be more approachable for women

   c. women are only buying from companies that respect them

   d. artists could stop producing fashionable products if they feel bullied

Questions 13 - 16 refer to the following passage.

FDR, the Treaty of Versailles, and the Fourteen Points

At the conclusion of World War I, those who had won the war and those who were forced to admit defeat welcomed the end of the war and expected that a peace treaty would be signed. The American president, Franklin D. Roosevelt, played an important part in proposing what the agreements should be and did so through his Fourteen Points.
World War I had begun in 1914 when an Austrian archduke was assassinated, leading to a domino effect that pulled the world's most powerful countries into war on a large scale. The war catalysed the creation and use of deadly weapons that had not previously existed, resulting in a great loss of soldiers on both sides of the fighting. More than 9 million soldiers were killed.

The United States agreed to enter the war right before it ended, and many believed that its decision to become finally involved brought on the end of the war. FDR made it very clear that the U.S. was entering the war for moral reasons and had an agenda focused on world peace. The Fourteen Points were individual goals and ideas (focused on peace, free trade, open communication, and self-reliance) that FDR wanted the power nations to strive for now that the war had ended. He was optimistic and had many ideas about what could be accomplished through, and during the post-war peace. However, FDR's fourteen points were poorly received when he presented them to the leaders of other world powers, many of whom wanted only to help their own countries and to punish the Germans for fuelling the war, and they fell by the wayside. World War II was imminent, for Germany lost everything.

Some historians believe that the other leaders who participated in the Treaty of Versailles weren't receptive to the Fourteen Points because World War I was fought almost entirely on European soil, and the United States lost much less than did the other powers. FDR was in a unique position to determine the fate of the war, but doing it on his own terms did not help accomplish his goals. This is only one historical example of how the United State has tried to use its power as an important country, but found itself limited because of geological or ideological factors.

13. The main idea of this passage is that

a. World War I was unfair because no fighting took place in America

b. World War II happened because of the Treaty of Versailles

c. the power the United States has to help other countries also prevents it from helping other countries

d. Franklin D. Roosevelt was one of the United States' smartest presidents

14. According to the second paragraph, World War I started because

a. an archduke was assassinated

b. weapons that were more deadly had been developed

c. a domino effect of allies agreeing to help each other

d. the world's most powerful countries were large

15. The author includes the detail that 9 million soldiers were killed

a. to demonstrate why European leaders were hesitant to accept peace

b. to show the reader the dangers of deadly weapons

c. to make the reader think about which countries lost the most soldiers

d. to demonstrate why World War II was imminent

16. According to this passage, catalysed means

   a. analyzed

   b. sped up

   c. invented

   d. funded

Questions 17 - 20 refer to the following passage.

Chocolate Chip Cookies

3/4 cup sugar
3/4 cup packed brown sugar
1 cup butter, softened
2 large eggs, beaten
1 teaspoon vanilla extract
2 1/4 cups all-purpose flour
1 teaspoon baking soda
3/4 teaspoon salt
2 cups semisweet chocolate chips
If desired, 1 cup chopped pecans, or chopped walnuts.
Preheat oven to 375 degrees.

Mix sugar, brown sugar, butter, vanilla and eggs in a large bowl. Stir in flour, baking soda, and salt. The dough will be very stiff.

Stir in chocolate chips by hand with a sturdy wooden spoon. Add the pecans, or other nuts, if desired. Stir until the chocolate chips and nuts are evenly dispersed.

Drop dough by rounded tablespoonfuls 2 inches apart onto a cookie sheet.

Bake 8 to 10 minutes, or, until light brown. Cookies may look underdone, but they will finish cooking after you take them out of the oven.

17. What is the correct order for adding these ingredients?

    a. Brown sugar, baking soda, chocolate chips
    b. Baking soda, brown sugar, chocolate chips
    c. Chocolate chips, baking soda, brown sugar
    d. Baking soda, chocolate chips, brown sugar

18. What does sturdy mean?

    a. Long
    b. Strong
    c. Short
    d. Wide

19. What does disperse mean?

    a. Scatter
    b. To form a ball
    c. To stir
    d. To beat

20. When can you stop stirring the nuts?

    a. When the cookies are cooked.
    b. When the nuts are evenly distributed.
    c. When the nuts are added.
    d. After the chocolate chips are added.

Questions 21 - 23 refer to the following passage.

Lowest Price Guarantee

Get it for less. Guaranteed!

ABC Electric will beat any advertised price by 10% of the difference.

1) If you find a lower advertised price, we will beat it by 10% of the difference.

2) If you find a lower advertised price within 30 days* of your purchase we will beat it by 10% of the difference.

3) If our own price is reduced within 30 days* of your purchase, bring in your receipt and we will refund the difference.

*14 days for computers, monitors, printers, laptops, tablets, cellular & wireless devices, home security products, projectors, camcorders, digital cameras, radar detectors, portable DVD players, DJ and pro-audio equipment, and air conditioners.

21. I bought a radar detector 15 days ago and saw an ad for the same model only cheaper. Can I get 10% of the difference refunded?

    a. Yes. Since it is less than 30 days, you can get 10% of the difference refunded.

    b. No. Since it is more than 14 days, you cannot get 10% of the difference re-funded.

    c. It depends on the cashier.

    d. Yes. You can get the difference refunded.

22. I bought a flat-screen TV for $500 10 days ago and found an advertisement for the same TV, at another store, on sale for $400. How much will ABC refund under this guarantee?

    a. $100
    b. $110
    c. $10
    d. $400

23. What is the purpose of this passage?

   a. To inform
   b. To educate
   c. To persuade
   d. To entertain

Questions 24 - 27 refer to the following passage.

Passage 6 - What Is Mardi Gras?

Mardi Gras is fast becoming one of the South's most famous and most celebrated holidays. The word Mardi Gras comes from the French and the literal translation is "Fat Tuesday." The holiday has also been called Shrove Tuesday, due to its associations with Lent. The purpose of Mardi Gras is to celebrate and enjoy before the Lenten season of fasting and repentance begins.

What originated by the French Explorers in New Orleans, Louisiana in the 17th century is now celebrated all over the world. Panama, Italy, Belgium and Brazil all host large scale Mardi Gras celebrations, and many smaller cities and towns celebrate this fun loving Tuesday as well. Usually held in February or early March, Mardi Gras is a day of extravagance, a day for people to eat, drink and be merry, to wear costumes, masks and to dance to jazz music.
The French explorers on the Mississippi River would be in shock today if they saw the opulence of the parades and floats that grace the New Orleans streets during Mardi Gras these days. Parades in New Orleans are divided by organizations. These are more commonly known as Krewes.

Being a member of a Krewe is quite a task because Krewes are responsible for overseeing the parades. Each Krewe's parade is ruled by a Mardi Gras "King and Queen." The role of the King and Queen is to "bestow" gifts on their adoring fans as the floats ride along the street. They throw doubloons, which is fake money and usually colored green, purple and gold, which are the colors of Mardi Gras. Beads in those color shades are also thrown and cups are thrown as well.

Beads are by far the most popular souvenir of any Mardi Gras parade, with each spectator attempting to gather as many as possible.

24. The purpose of Mardi Gras is to

    a. Repent for a month.

    b. Celebrate in extravagant ways.

    c. Be a member of a Krewe.

    d. Explore the Mississippi.

25. From reading the passage we can infer that "Kings and Queens"

    a. Have to be members of a Krewe.

    b. Have to be French.

    c. Have to know how to speak French.

    d. Have to give away their own money.

26. Which group of people began to hold Mardi Gras celebrations?

    a. Settlers from Italy

    b. Members of Krewes

    c. French explorers

    d. Belgium explorers

27. In the context of the passage, what does the word spectator mean?

    a. Someone who participates actively

    b. Someone who watches the parade's action

    c. Someone on the parade floats

    d. Someone who does not celebrate Mardi Gras

Questions 28 - 30 refer to the following passage.

Passage 7 - The Life of Helen Keller

Many people have heard of Helen Keller. She is famous because she was unable to see or hear, but learned to speak and read and went onto attend college and earn a degree. Her life is a very interesting story, one that she developed into an autobiography, which was then adapted into both a stage play and a movie. How did Helen Keller overcome her disabilities to become a famous woman? Read on to find out. Helen Keller was not born blind and deaf. When she was a small baby, she had a very high fever for several days. As a result of her sudden illness, baby Helen lost her eyesight and her hearing. Because she was so young when she went deaf and blind, Helen Keller never had any recollection of being able to see or hear. Since she could not hear, she could not learn to talk. Since she could not see, it was difficult for her to move around. For the first six years of her life, her world was very still and dark.

Imagine what Helen's childhood was like. She could not hear her mother's voice. She could not see the beauty of her parent's farm. She could not recognize who was giving her a hug, or a bath or even where her bedroom was each night. Worse, she could not communicate with her parents in any way. She could not express her feelings or tell them the things she wanted. It must have been a very sad childhood.

When Helen was six years old, her parents hired her a teacher named Anne Sullivan. Anne was a young woman who was almost blind. However, she could hear and she could read Braille, so she was a perfect teacher for young Helen. At first, Anne had a very hard time teaching Helen anything. She described her first impression of Helen as a "wild thing, not a child." Helen did not like Anne at first either. She bit and hit Anne when Anne tried to teach her. However, the two of them eventually came to have a great deal of love and respect.

Anne taught Helen to hear by putting her hands on people's throats. She could feel the sounds people made. In time,

Helen learned to feel what people said. Next, Anne taught Helen to read Braille, which is a way that books are written for the blind. Finally, Anne taught Helen to talk. Although Helen did learn to talk, it was hard for anyone but Anne to understand her.

As Helen grew older, she amazed more and more people with her story. She went to college and wrote books about her life. She gave talks to the public, with Anne at her side, translating her words. Today, both Anne Sullivan and Helen Keller are famous women who are respected for their lives' work.

28. Helen Keller could not see and hear and so, what was her biggest problem in childhood?

    a. Inability to communicate

    b. Inability to walk

    c. Inability to play

    d. Inability to eat

29. Helen learned to hear by feeling the vibrations people made when they spoke. What were these vibrations were felt through?

    a. Mouth

    b. Throat

    c. Ears

    d. Lips

30. From the passage, we can infer that Anne Sullivan was a patient teacher. We can infer this because

    a. Helen hit and bit her and Anne remained her teacher.

    b. Anne taught Helen to read only.

    c. Anne was hard of hearing too.

    d. Anne wanted to be a teacher.

Listening Comprehension

Directions: Scan the QR code below with any smartphone or tablet for an audio recording of the listening comprehension passages below. Or, have someone read them to you. Listen carefully to the passages and answer the questions that follow.

What is a QR Code?
A QR code looks like a barcode and it's used as a shortcut to link to content online using your phone's camera, saving you from typing lengthy addresses into your mobile browser.

Questions 1 - 3 refer to the following passage.

Passage 1 - Common Causes of household fires

It's hard to believe, but the most common causes of house fires are the most common things in houses. This is because we use fire, or electricity daily, as part of our regular routine; cooking, heating water in water heaters, decorative candles and in many other ways. Another thing people don't usually consider is that electrical failures can cause a fire.

Most fires start in the kitchen when a pot on the stove is left unattended. Even something as simple as a pot with boiling water can be dangerous: if the water spills from the pot and extinguishes the fire in the burner, and the propane gas spreads through the kitchen. After this, it only needs a spark to start a fire.

If there is someone there that can turn off the gas, or get the burner going again, there will be no hazard. So, the kitchen mustn't be left unattended as a precaution.

Electricity can cause a fire in many ways; an electrical short, a damaged wire, an overloaded power circuit, an over-heated hair dryer or even for poor installation of equipment. So, it's important to make every installation properly done and that they get adequate maintenance. Poor installation of house wiring can be especially dangerous. Therefore there are so many regulations regarding the electrical installation.

Smoking is another major cause of fires. A cigarette in bed can light the sheets and start a fire, a half-burned but falling on the carpet can also start a fire.

Scan for Audio or click
https://www.test-preparation.ca/audio/HouseHoldFires.mp3

1. Why are household fires so common?

    a. Faulty wiring

    b. Because we use fire so often

    c. Household fires are not common

    d. A lot of people smoke

2. Where so most fires start?

    a. the kitchen

    b. the bedroom

    c. the living room

    d. the basement

3. What is a major cause of fires besides electricity and fire?

    a. Power tools

    b. Smoking

    c. Pets

    d. Laptops

Questions 4 - 6 refer to the following passage.

News story #1

This weekend a home in Brooklyn burst into flames while the owners where downtown. The young couple, Mary and John Smith left their home Saturday morning, after a quick breakfast, and went downtown to spend the day. But the day was interrupted at noon by a call from the couples' upstairs neighbor, who said that he smelled smoke, called the fire department, and that their apartment was in flames. When Mary and John got home, the fire department had put out the fire, and there was only ashes.

The preliminary assessment of the fire department indicated the fire was started by candles left on a desk, near papers on a big bookshelf. Also, the department had no fire security system to warn of the smoke. The regulations regarding home fire security stated that lit candles can't be left unattended, so the fire department declared the fire was causes by negligence. With this, the insurance company can deny to responsibility in the terrible accident.

Scan for audio or click
https://www.test-preparation.ca/audio/News1.mp3

4. Where were the owners when the fire started?

    a. At home

    b. Visiting their friend upstairs

    c. Downtown for the day

    d. In the backyard

5. What started the fire?

    a. Candles left burning near some papers

    b. We don't know the cause

    c. The flames started from cooking breakfast

    d. The upstairs neighbor

6. Did their home burn down completely?

    a. Yes

    b. No

    c. We cannot tell from the story

Questions 7 - 9 refer to the following passage.

News story #2

This is a story about a hero without a cape: an 18-year-old boy rescued a baby and an elderly woman from a burning house.

On his way to school Tom Pitt noticed smoke coming out of a house near his home. As he approached the smoking house, he noticed that the house was on fire and heard screams coming from the inside. The teenager immediately called the emergency service and gave the address. But the house is a bit outside the city, so he knew that it would take a while before the fire department got there.

The young hero ran into the blazing house, rescuing a one-year old baby girl and then coming back to rescue her 83-year-old grandmother. They were trapped inside the fire, which presumably started because the granny fell asleep, leaving the oven ON. The young hero, Tom Pitt, was awarded with the keys to the city for his amazing rescue, risking his life to save others.

Scan for audio or click
https://www.test-preparation.ca/audio/News2.mp3

7. Where was Tom going when he noticed the burning house?

    a. He was at home

    b. He was going to school

    c. He was going home

    d. He was going downtown

8. What did Tom do when he saw the house was on fire?

    a. He went into rescue the baby and grandmother

    b. He called the emergency services

    c. He went home to call the emergency services

    d. None of the above

9. Why did it take a long time for the firefighters to arrive?

    a. The fire department was busy

    b. It did not take a long time

    c. I take a long time because the house was out of town

    d. None of the above

Questions 10 - 11 refer to the following passage.

Volcanoes

A volcano is a split in the plates that compose the surface of a planet. A split in the plates, allows gases, lava and volcanic ashes in magma chambers deep below the Earth to surface, when the volcano erupts. There are many volcanoes on planet Earth. Most volcanos are underwater. Volcanoes are the natural way that the Earth has of releasing internal heat and pressure. A volcano erupts when the pressure of the magma below the surface is greater than the rocks surrounding it.

Scan for audio or click
https://www.test-preparation.ca/audio/Volcano.mp3

10. Where are most volcanoes?

    a. Underwater

    b. On land

    c. In Europe

    d. In the US

11. What causes volcanoes?

    a. Magma

    b. A split in the earth's plates

    c. Escaping gas

    c. None of the above

Questions 12 - 15 refer to the following passage.

Types of Volcanoes

One of the biggest tragedies in the history of mankind occurred when the volcano Vesuvius erupted and covered The roman city of Pompeii with lava and toxic gases in minutes. But despite its dangers, they are a necessary process that the Earth uses to balance itself.

There are many types of volcanoes, many are underwater, others over the surface; some have constant small eruptions, some other haven't erupted in centuries; some have conical form, others are narrow. For example, shield volcanoes are common in the Hawaiian volcanic chain. Shield volcanoes are volcanoes with small explosions of a low-viscosity lava that can flow long distances. There are also volcanoes called lava domes. Unlike shield volcanoes, these have highly viscous lava that covers the mountain. There are as well Stratovolcanoes, which are tall conical mountains formed of lava flows, so they are shaped during different eruptions.

The terrible super-volcanoes are capable of destruction on a continental scale. Due to the enormous volume of ashes and sulfuric vapors, they can even cool the global temperature for years after the eruption. Underwater volcanoes are very common on the ocean floor. They don't usually have big explosions due to the enormous weight and pressure of the water, which prevents the gases from being released.

Scan for audio or click
https://www.test-preparation.ca/audio/TypesVolcano.mp3

12. What happened when Vesuvius erupted?

   a. It covered the city of Pompeii

   b. It cooled the global temperature

   c. It was not a big explosion

   d. None of the above

13. Where are Shield Volcanoes commonly found?

   a. In the Arctic

   b. In Russia

   c. In the Hawaiian Islands

   d. In Canada

14. What are Stratovolcanoes?

   a. Super-volcanoes

   b. Conical mountains of lava

   c. Underwater volcanoes

   d. Lava domes

15. Do underwater volcanoes have big explosions?

   a. Yes

   b. No

   d. None of the above

Mathematics

1. 8327 – 1278 =

    a. 7149
    b. 7209
    c. 6059
    d. 7049

2. 294 X 21 =

    a. 6017
    b. 6174
    c. 6728
    d. 5679

3. 1278 + 4920 =

    a. 6298
    b. 6108
    c. 6198
    d. 6098

4. 285 * 12 =

    a. 3420
    b. 3402
    c. 3024
    d. 2322

5. 4120 – 3216 =

    a. 903
    b. 804
    c. 904
    d. 1904

6. 2417 + 1004 =

    a. 3401
    b. 4321
    c. 3402
    d. 3421

7. 1440 ÷ 12 =

    a. 122
    b. 120
    c. 110
    d. 132

8. 2713 – 1308 =

    a. 1450
    b. 1445
    c. 1405
    d. 1455

9. The length of a rectangle is 5 in. more than its width. The perimeter of the rectangle is 26 in. What is the width and length of the rectangle?

    a. width = 6 inches, Length = 9 inches
    b. width = 4 inches, Length = 9 inches
    c. width = 4 inches, Length = 5 inches
    d. width = 6 inches, Length = 11 inches

10. Kate's father is 32 years older than Kate is. In 5 years, he will be five times older. How old is Kate?

   a. 2
   b. 3
   c. 5
   d. 6

11. A store owner buys merchandise for $21,045. He transports them for $3,905 and pays his staff $1,450 to stock the merchandise on his shelves. If he does not incur further costs, how much does he need to sell the items to make $5,000 profit?

   a. $32,500
   b. $29,350
   c. $32,400
   d. $31,400

12. A basket contains 125 oranges, mangos and apples. If 3/5 of the fruits in the basket are mangos and only 2/5 of the mangos are ripe, how many ripe mangos are there in the basket?

   a. 30
   b. 68
   c. 55
   d. 47

13. Employees of a discount appliance store receive an additional 20% off the lowest price on any item. If an employee purchases a dishwasher during a 15% off sale, how much will he pay if the dishwasher originally cost $450?

   a. $280.90
   b. $287.00
   c. $292.50
   d. $306.00

14. The sale price of a car is $12,590, which is 20% off the original price. What is the original price?

    a. $14,310.40
    b. $14,990.90
    c. $15,108.00
    d. $15,737.50

15. A goat eats 214 kg. of hay in 60 days, while a cow eats the same amount in 15 days. How long will it take them to eat this hay together?

    a. 37.5
    b. 75
    c. 12
    d. 15

16. Express 25% as a fraction.

    a. 1/4
    b. 7/40
    c. 6/25
    d. 8/28

17. Express 125% as a decimal.

    a. .125
    b. 12.5
    c. 1.25
    d. 125

18. Solve for x: 30 is 40% of x

    a. 60
    b. 90
    c. 85
    d. 75

19. 12 ½% of x is equal to 50. Solve for x.

   a. 300
   b. 400
   c. 450
   d. 350

20. Express 24/56 as a reduced common fraction.

   a. 4/9
   b. 4/11
   c. 3/7
   d. 3/8

21. Express 87% as a decimal.

   a. .087
   b. 8.7
   c. .87
   d. 87

22. 60 is 75% of x. Solve for x.

   a. 80
   b. 90
   c. 75
   d. 70

23. 60% of x is 12. Solve for x.

   a. 18
   b. 15
   c. 25
   d. 20

24. Express 71/1000 as a decimal.

    a. .71

    b. .0071

    c. .071

    d. 7.1

25. 4.7 + .9 + .01 =

    a. 5.5

    b. 6.51

    c. 5.61

    d. 5.7

26. .84 ÷ .7 =

    a. .12

    b. 12

    c. .012

    d. 1.2

27. What number is in the ten thousandths place in 1.7389?

    a. 1

    b. 8

    c. 9

    d. 3

28. .87 - .48 =

    a. .39

    b. .49

    c. .41

    d. .37

29. Convert 60 feet to inches.

   a. 700 inches

   b. 600 inches

   c. 720 inches

   d. 1,800 inches

30. Convert 25 centimeters to millimeters.

   a. 250 millimeters

   b. 7.5 millimeters

   c. 5 millimeters

   d. 2.5 millimeters

Part IV - Mechanical Comprehension

1. Which of the following is true of the relationship between screws and threads?

   a. The larger the distance between threads, the easier to turn.

   b. The smaller the distance between threads, the easier to turn.

   c. The smaller the distance between threads, the more difficult to turn.

   d. None of the above

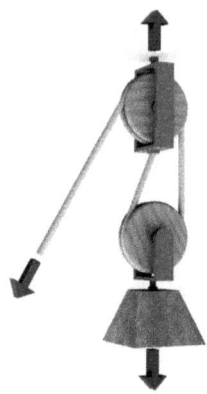

2. Consider the arrangement of pulleys above. If the weight shown is 150 pounds, how much force much be exerted to lift the weight?

    a. 150 pounds
    b. 100 pounds
    c. 75 pounds
    d. 50 pounds

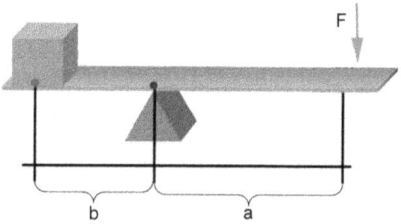

3. Consider the illustration above and the corresponding data:

Weight = W = 100 pounds
Distance from fulcrum to Weight = b = 5 feet
Distance from fulcrum to point where force is applied = a = 10 feet
How much force (F) must be applied to lift the weight?

a. 100
b. 50
c. 25
d. 10

4. Consider a gear train with 3 gears, from left to right, A with 10 teeth, gear B with 40 teeth, and gear C with 10 teeth. Gear A turns clockwise at 80 rpm. What direction and speed in rpm does Gear C turn?

a. 100 rpm, clockwise
b. 80 rpm clockwise
c. 120 rpm counter clockwise
d. 100 rpm counter clockwise

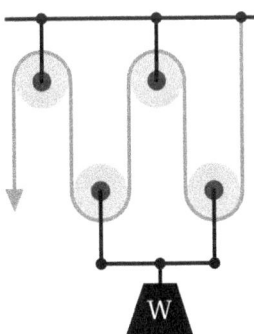

5. Consider the pulley arrangement above. If the weight, W, is 100 pounds, then how much force is required to lift the weight?

a. 100 pounds
b. 50 pounds
c. 25 pounds
d. 20 pounds

6. A cam is a mechanical linkage that:

a. Transforms linear motion into rotary motion and vice versa.

b. Transforms oscillating motion in to linear motion and vice versa.

c. Transforms reciprocating motion to oscillating motion.

d. None of the above

7. What is the function of a crankshaft?

a. To transform the back-and-forth motion of the pistons into rotary motion.

b. To transform rotary motion into reciprocal motion.

c. To transfer the rotary motion of the cam to the wheels

d. None of the above.

8. Consider two meshed gears, one that is twice as large as the other. How fast will the smaller gear rotate?

a. One-quarter as fast as the larger gear

b. Twice as fast as the larger gear

c. 50% faster than the larger gear

d. None of the above

9. What does a tachometer measure?

a. A tachometer measures rotation speed

b. A tachometer measures temperature

c. A tachometer measures pressure

d. A tachometer measures speed

10. Which of the following best describes an allen wrench?

    a. An l-shaped wrench with 5 sides

    b. An l-shaped wrench with 6 sides

    c. An l-shaped wrench with 4 sides

    d. None of the above

11. What tool is used to tighten bits in an electric drill?

    a. Chuck

    b. Tang

    c. Allen Wrench

    d. None of the above

12. How many hydrants are on Los Feliz Blvd?

    a. 1

    b. 2

    c. 3

    d. 4

13. Taking the shortest route from Golden State Fwy 5 and Los Felix, to Santa Monica Blvd and Versont, how many corners are there?

    a. 1
    b. 2
    c. 3
    d. 4

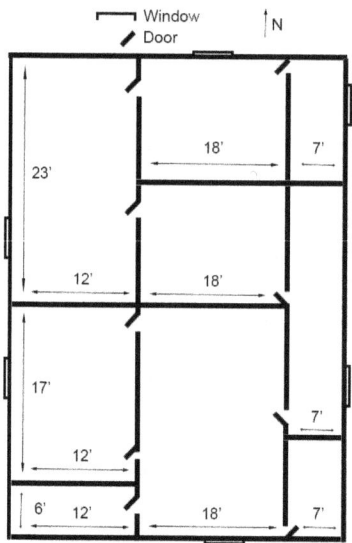

14. What is the width of this house from west to east?

    a. 47
    b. 37
    c. 46
    d. 48

15. What is the length of this house from north to south?

    a. 47
    b. 37
    c. 46
    d. 48

16. Which of the following represent an overhead view of the house below?

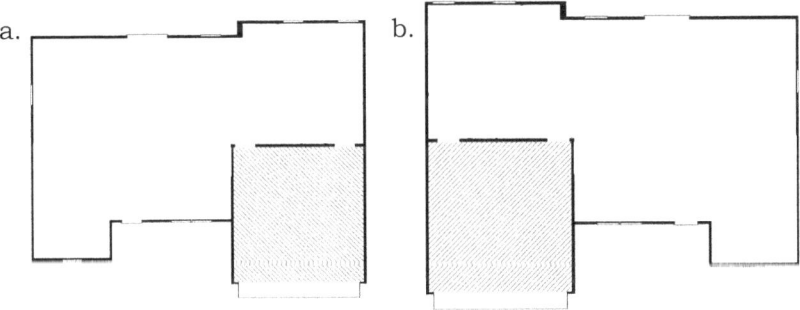

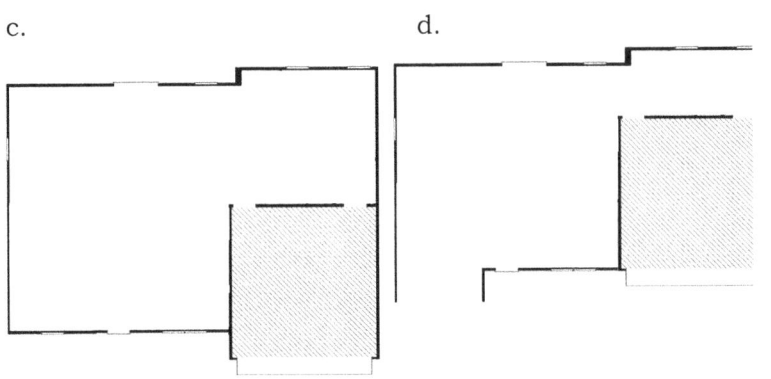

17. Which of the following represent an overhead view of the house below?

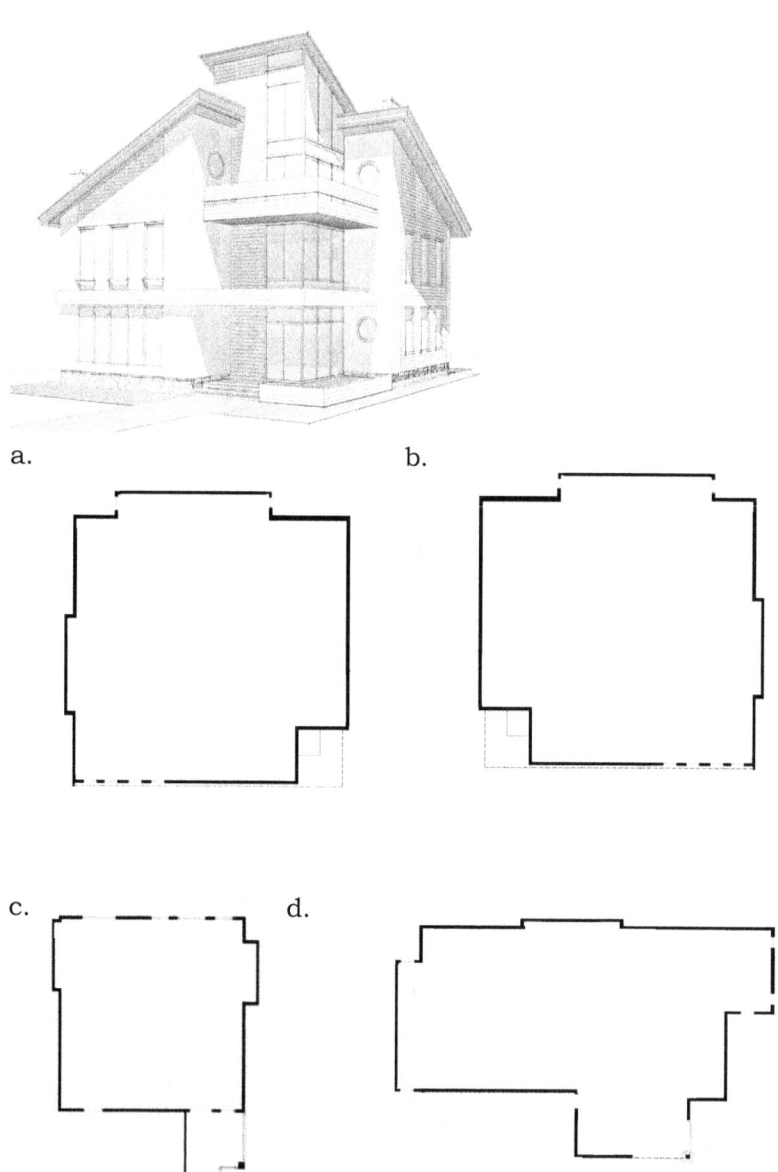

18. Which of the following illustrates the principal of the lever?

    a. The greater the distance over which the force is applied, the greater the force required (to lift the load).

    b. The greater the distance over which the force is applied, the smaller the force required (to lift the load).

    c. The smaller the distance over which the force is applied, the smaller the force required (to lift the load).

    d. None of the above

19. What is the value of the force F enough to lift the object up, if the weight W of the object is 360 N?

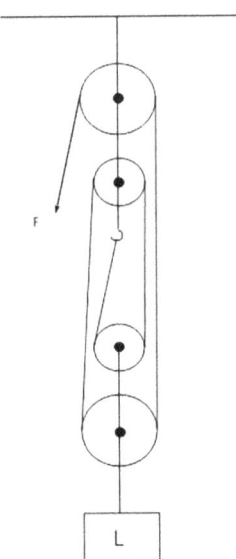

    a. 180 N
    b. 120 N
    c. 90 N
    d. 72 N

20. How many turns does gear 1 make when gear 3 makes 210 turns?

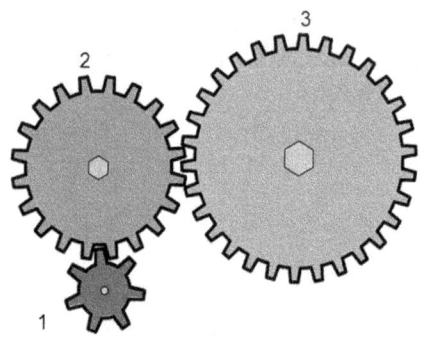

   a. 30
   b. 90
   c. 300
   d. 900

Mapping

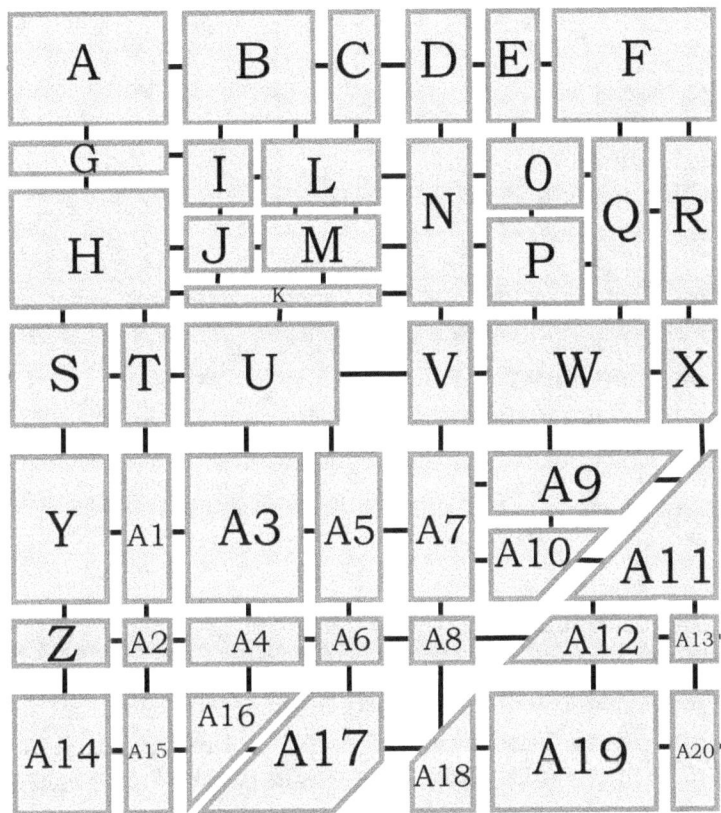

Map Key

Each Square labeled A to Z and A1 to A20 represent the corner of an intersection. The lines between the squares represent a city block. The intersections and city blocks fall into 3 categories.

Large blocks: A, B,F, H, N, Q, R, U, W, Y, A3, A5, A7, A9, A11, A14, A17, A19

Small blocks: C, D, E, I. J, L,M, O, P, S, T, V, X, A1, A4, A10, Z, A12, A15, A16, A18, A20

Mini blocks: G, K, A2, A6, A8, A13

The time it takes to travel from one city block to another is:

Large blocks

In a car: 4 minutes
On a bike: 6 minutes
On foot: 10 minutes

Small Blocks

In a car: 3 minutes
On a bike: 5 minutes
On foot: 8 minutes

Mini Blocks

In a car: 2 minutes
On a bike: 4 minutes
On foot: 6 minutes

1. A girl rides a bike from A12 to A5 and returns to A12 by a different route. How long would it take?

    a. 35 minutes

    b. 37 minutes

    c. 39 minutes

    d. 28 minutes

2. There is a parade and block O is closed to vehicles. A driver starts at block N and drives to R. Then he has to return to N by a different route. How fast could he accomplish this?

    a. 20 minutes

    b. 11 minutes

    c. 27 minutes

    d. 25 minutes

3. A man rides a bike from A18 to block N and then returns via the same route. How long would it take him if he used the fastest route?

   a. 41 minutes
   b. 38 minutes
   c. 44 minutes
   d. 29 minutes

4. A police patrol team drove from A3 to A10, with a 30 seconds stop at each intersection in between. From A10 it then drove to block W without spending any extra time at the intersections. How long would the trip take using the fastest route?

   a. 19 minutes, 30 seconds
   b. 18 minutes
   c. 20 minutes
   d. 21 minutes, 45 seconds

5. A delivery van goes from block U to A4. How fast would it take, it if it had to go through block V and spend an extra 15 seconds each time it has to make a turn at an intersection?

   a. 15 minutes, 30 seconds
   b. 15 minutes, 15 seconds
   c. 17 minutes, 30 seconds
   d. 16 minutes, 30 seconds

6. A group of 4 students move from block F to block A. How fast can they go if they drive a car the first 2 blocks, ride their bikes the next 2 blocks and walk the rest of the way?

   a. 25 minutes
   b. 27 minutes
   c. 30 minutes
   d. 29 minutes

7. A car drives from block R to A10. Using the fastest route, how long would it take if it spends 30 seconds each time it has to turn at an intersection?

    a. 6 minutes

    b. 7 minutes

    c. 10 minutes, 30 seconds

    d. 7 minutes, 30 seconds

8. Using the fastest route, a bike ride from V to A18 and then a car ride to A4 through A16 would take how long?

    a. 25 minutes

    b. 22 minutes

    c. 28 minutes

    d. 24 minutes

9. A boy rides his bike from S to K but gets lost along the way. What is the shortest time it would have taken him if his trip took him through blocks J and L?

    a. 20 minutes

    b. 22 minutes

    c. 23 minutes

    d. 25 minutes

10. Which of the following would be the shortest trip?

    a. Bike ride from D to V

    b. Walking from O to W

    c. Driving a car from B to A3

    d. They all take the same time

11. A bike race starts from block U and finishes at block A18. If the race has to pass through blocks V and A6, what is the shortest possible time to complete the race?

   a. 29 minutes
   b. 34 minutes
   c. 30 minutes
   d. 31 minutes

12. There is traffic congestion around blocks N, V, A7 and A8. Cars can't get through, and drivers need to park and walk. A car driver heads for block A12 from U. How quickly can they get there?

   a. 19 minutes
   b. 17 minutes
   c. 21 minutes
   d. 18 minutes

13. How long will it take to walk from block T to block A15 if you must walk through A16?

   a. 38 minutes
   b. 41 minutes
   c. 42 minutes
   d. 37 minutes

14. How long will it take to drive a car from S to W?

   a. 6 minutes
   b. 12 minutes
   c. 18 minutes
   d. 13 minutes

15. How long to ride a bike from block G to block O?

   a. 24 minutes
   b. 19 minutes
   c. 20 minutes
   d. 21 minutes

Situation Judgment

Scenario 1

A new team member seems hesitant to ask for help. How can you support them?

   a. Wait for them to approach you.
   b. Offer your assistance and let them know you are available.
   c. Assume they will figure it out on their own.
   d. Criticize them for not asking for help.

Scenario 2

During a project, you and a colleague have a disagreement on the approach to take. How should you resolve it?

   a. Insist on your approach and disregard theirs.
   b. Discuss both approaches and find a compromise.
   c. Avoid the colleague and proceed with your plan.
   d. Report the disagreement to the supervisor immediately.

Scenario 3

You receive feedback from a team member that your communication style is too direct. How should you respond?

a. Dismiss their feedback and continue as usual.

b. Reflect on their feedback and adjust your communication style.

c. Argue that your style is effective and doesn't need change.

d. Avoid communicating with that team member in the future.

Scenario 4

Some of your team members are less committed than in the recent past.

How should you go about improving commitment?

a. Introduce work incentives.

b. Reduce compensation for the employees who are not producing.

c. Talk to the employees on the need of being committed.

d. Fire the team and get another team.

Scenario 5

You overhear discussions during coffee break about your planned termination. However, you feel that you are being wrongfully accused.

How would you react in such a situation?

    a. Explain your side of the story.

    b. Accuse other employees.

    c. Blame the company.

    d. Accept defeat and go home.

Scenario 6

You are required to collaborate with a coworker who is tough to please. For the success of the project, both of you need to work together. What is the first step dealing with this situation?

    a. Stay calm and try to understand their point of view.

    b. Demean them and disregard their input.

    c. Report to your supervisor that you can't work with them.

    d. Ignore their unhelpful behavior.

Scenario 7

Your colleague has recently been criticized for poor performance. You need to do something to uplift their spirits.

How should you go about this?

    a. Criticize his weaknesses.

    b. Tell of his critics.

    c. Show that you care.

    d. Encourage them to learn from their mistakes.

Scenario 8

In the past, your department has been commended for excellent performance. You notice one of your team members is distracted, distressed and falling behind.

How would you address this issue?

    a. Refer him to the guidance and counseling team.

    b. Actively listen to his problems and compare them with yours.

    c. Report this matter to your supervisor.

    d. Actively listen and advise him to the best of your ability.

Scenario 9

You are a supervisor where one of your juniors is a close friend to your manager and talks to the manager about your projects before you get a chance to report. This embarrasses you as he exaggerates the potential risks.

What should you do?

    a. Befriend the employee and establish better ground rules

    b. Ask your boss to only share information with you

    c. Maneuver the employee into difficult situations that cause poor performance and fire them

    d. Isolate this employee so they have less impact on your team

Scenario 10

You have the responsibility to read through an intern's draft report and have discovered the report does not meet any of the objectives set. You have limited time to improve the report before presenting it to your client.

What should you do?

>a. Let your intern find out what happens when a client receives a sub-standard report.
>
>b. Forward the draft report to other analysts in your department for their own comments.
>
>c. Ask your own manager what would have happened if you hadn't checked this report.
>
>d. Email your collated amends to the intern; offering to explain each one in further detail.

Scenario 11

You are a busy team leader attending a meeting where the presenter has overrun the allocated time. You agree that the presentation is going on for too long.

What should you do?

>a. Leave the meeting and explain you have an urgent matter to attend to.
>
>b. Wrap up the session then set up a presentation review later.
>
>c. Wrap-up the session by secretly messaging the whole team to ask questions.
>
>d. Leave time management to the presenter as it is his/her responsibility.

Scenario 12

You have been working in the same company for 3 years and have successfully risen through the ranks. You now have the feeling that you have reached your potential in the company and start pursuing options to advance your career in other organizations. You are currently negotiating a new contract and rumors that you are switching jobs are spreading fast in your company.

What should you do?

a. You decide that since the rumor is already out, you update everyone of your ongoing negotiations in the new company. You do this as it may even push your current directors to give you a promotion in the current company.

b. Since nothing has been decided yet and it is still a rumor you maintain your silence on the issue until you give notice.

c. Since you will probably leave and the rumor is already out, you invest less and less in your current position and invest more time in getting the new position.

d. Since the rumor is out, you address your manager's doubts by updating him of your intentions of leaving and keep working normally since you are still an employee.

Scenario 13

You are being undermined by a co-worker that has a junior position to you and has not been working there as long as you. He is, however, considered a fast learner and is more educated than you. You get information from someone that the co-worker is interested in taking over your some of your roles.

What should you do?

a. Wait to see how it turns out as all this is hearsay and you consider it rumors.

b. You call the co-worker and talk to them, letting them know that cooperation is essential in any organization and you have something to learn form each other. You say that you will take more serious action if he refuses to understand.

c. You treat the matter with seriousness taking no chances. Your report your co-worker to your supervisor and advise him to replace the co-worker.

d. Since you don't want to turn the matter into a big issue, you seek the help of a third party in telling your co-worker that their behavior cannot be tolerated.

Scenario 14

You are assigned a joint project with a co-worker who has been working in the department longer than you have. He does not put in much effort as he lacks the motivation to develop professionally.

What should you do?

a. You accept the situation as it is and share the workload to the best of your ability. You leave the rest up to him.

b. You are concerned that poor quality work will effect your reputation and the company's reputation negatively and decide to put in extra hours to complete personally the project in the best way you can.

c. You contact your manger to report the situation as you cannot tolerate this attitude. You request the co-worker be replaced for the project.

d. You talk to the co-worker and negotiate that the work be distributed fairly between the two of you. You however consider the fact that you might have to put in extra effort to complete the project.

Scenario 15

Your phone completely breaks down while talking to client leaving them hanging.

What should you do?

a. Email your manager informing them of the situation and ask what they would do.

b. Call the customer from your personal phone, apologizing that they were cut-off

c. Send the customer an email and ask if they can talk to you using a live communication platform.

d. Get a colleague to call the customer on your behalf and ask them to explain the situation.

Answer Key

1. A

Choice B is incorrect; the author did not express their opinion on the subject matter. Choice C is incorrect, the author was not trying to prove a point.

2. C

Choice C is correct; historians believe it was brutal and bloody. Choice A is incorrect; there is no consensus that the Crusades achieved great things. Choice B is incorrect; it did not stabilize the Holy Lands. Choice D is incorrect, some historians do believe this was the purpose but not all historians.

3. D

The feudal system led to infighting. Choice A is incorrect, it had the opposite effect. Choice B is incorrect, though this is a good answer, it is not the best answer. The Church asked for volunteers not the Feudal Lords. Choice C is incorrect, it did have an effect on the Crusades.

4. A

Saracen was a generic term for Muslims widely used in Europe during the later medieval era.

5. B

This warranty does not cover a product that you have tried to fix yourself. From paragraph two, "This limited warranty does not cover ... any unauthorized disassembly, repair, or modification. "

6. C

ABC Electric could either replace or repair the fan, provided the other conditions are met. ABC Electric has the option to repair or replace.

7. B

The warranty does not cover a stove damaged in a flood. From the passage, "This limited warranty does not cover any damage to the product from improper installation, accident, abuse, misuse, natural disaster, insufficient or excessive electrical supply, abnormal mechanical or environmental conditions."

A flood is an "abnormal environmental condition," and a natural disaster, so it is not covered.

8. A
A missing part is an example of defective workmanship. This is an error made in the manufacturing process. A defective part is not considered workmanship.

9. D
This question tests the reader's summarization skills. The other choices A, B, and C focus on portions of the second paragraph that are too narrow and do not relate to the specific portion of text in question. The complexity of the sentence may mislead students into selecting one of these answers, but rearranging or restating the sentence will lead the reader to the correct answer. In addition, choice A makes an assumption that may or may not be true about the intentions of the company, choice B focuses on one product rather than the idea of the products, and choice C makes an assumption about women that may or may not be true and is not supported by the text.

10. B
This question tests reader's attention to detail. If a reader selects A, he or she may have picked up on the use of the word "debate" and assumed, very logically, that the two are at odds because they are fighting; however, this is simply not supported in the text. Choice C also uses very specific quotes from the text, but it rearranges and gives them false meaning. The artists want to elevate their creations above the creations of other artists, thereby showing that they are "creative" and "innovative." Similarly, choice D takes phrases straight from the text and rearranges and confuses them. The artists are described as wanting to be "creative, innovative, individual people," not the women.

11. A
This question tests reader's vocabulary and summarization skills. This phrase, used by the author, may seem flippant and dismissive if readers focus on the word "whatever" and

misinterpret it as a popular, colloquial term. In this way, choices B and C may mislead the reader to selecting one of them by including the terms "unimportant" and "stupid," respectively. Choice D is a similar misreading, but doesn't make sense when the phrase is at the beginning of the passage and the entire passage is on media messages. Choice A is literally and contextually appropriate, and the reader can understand that the author would like to keep the introduction focused on the topic the passage is going to discuss.

12. A

This question tests a reader's inference skills. The extreme use of the word "all" in choice B suggests that every single advertising company are working to be approachable, and while this is not only unlikely, the text specifically states that "more" companies have done this, signifying that they have not all participated, even if it's a possibility that they may some day. The use of the limiting word "only" in choice C lends that answer similar problems; women are still buying from companies who do not care about this message, or those companies would not be in business, and the passage specifies that "many" women are worried about media messages, but not all. Readers may find choice D logical, especially if they are looking to make an inference, and while this may be a possibility, the passage does not suggest or discuss this happening. Choice A is correct based on specifically because of the relation between "still working" in the answer and "will hopefully" and the extensive discussion on companies struggles, which come only with progress, in the text.

13. C

This question tests the reader's summarization skills. The entire passage is leading up to the idea that the president of the US may not have had grounds to assert his Fourteen Points when other countries had lost so much. Choice A is pretty directly inferred by the text, but it does not adequately summarize what the entire passage is trying to communicate. Choice B may also be inferred by the passage when it says that the war is "imminent," but it does not represent the entire message, either. The passage does seem to be in praise of FDR, or at least in respect of him, but it does not in any way claim that he is the smartest president, nor does this represent the many other points included. Choice C is then the obvious answer, and most directly relates to the closing sentences which it rewords.

14. C
This question tests the reader's attention to detail. The passage does state that choices A and B are true, and while those statements are in proximity to the explanation for why the war started, they are not the reason given. Choice D is a mix up of words used in the passage, which says that the largest powers were in play but not that this fact somehow started the war. The passage does make a direct statement that a domino effect started the war, supporting choice C as the correct answer.

15. A
This question tests the reader's understanding of functions in writing. Throughout the passage, it states that leaders of other nations were hesitant to accept generous or peaceful terms because of the grievances of the war, and the great loss of life was chief among these. While the passage does touch on the devastation of deadly weapons (B), the use of this raw, emotional fact serves a much larger purpose, and the focus of the passage is not the weapons. While readers may indeed consider who lost the most soldiers (C) when, so many countries were involved and the inequalities of loss are mentioned in the passage, there is no discussion of this in the passage. Choice D is related to A, but choice A is more direct and relates more to the passage.

16. B
This question tests the reader's vocabulary skills. Choice A may seem appealing to readers because it is phonetically similar to "catalysed," but the two are not related in any other way. Choice C makes sense in context, but if plugged in to the sentence creates a redundancy that doesn't make sense. Choice D does also not make sense contextually, even if the reader may consider that funds were needed to create more weaponry, especially if it was advanced.

17. A
The correct order of ingredients is brown sugar, baking soda and chocolate chips.

18. B
Sturdy: strong, solid in structure or person. In context, Stir in chocolate chips by hand with a *sturdy* wooden spoon.

19. A
Disperse: to scatter in different directions or break up. In context, Stir until the chocolate chips and nuts are evenly *dispersed*.

20. B
You can stop stirring the nuts when they are evenly distributed. From the passage, "Stir until the chocolate chips and nuts are evenly dispersed."

21. B
The time limit for radar detectors is 14 days. Since you made the purchase 15 days ago, you do not qualify for the guarantee.

22. B
Since you made the purchase 10 days ago, you are covered by the guarantee. Since it is an advertised price at a different store, ABC Electric will "beat" the price by 10% of the difference, which is,

500 − 400 = 100 − difference in price

100 X 10% = $10 − 10% of the difference

The advertised lower price is $400. ABC will beat this price by 10% so they will refund $100 + 10 = $110.

23. C
The purpose of this passage is to persuade.

24. B
The correct answer can be found in the fourth sentence of the first paragraph.

Choice A is incorrect because repenting begins the day AFTER Mardi Gras. Choice C is incorrect because you can celebrate Mardi Gras without being a member of a Krewe.

Choice D is incorrect because exploration does not play any

role in a modern Mardi Gras celebration.

25. A

The second sentence is the last paragraph states that Krewes are led by the Kings and Queens. Therefore, you must have to be part of a Krewe to be its King or its Queen.

Choice B is incorrect because it never states in the passage that only people from France can be Kings and Queen of Mardi Gras

Choice C is incorrect because the passage says nothing about having to speak French.

Choice D is incorrect because the passage does state that the Kings and Queens throw doubloons, which is fake money.

26. C

The first sentences of BOTH the 2nd and 3rd paragraphs mention that French explorers started this tradition in New Orleans.
Choices A, B and D are incorrect because they are names of cities or countries listed in the 2nd paragraph.

27. B

In the final paragraph, the word spectator is used to describe people who are watching the parade and catching cups, beads and doubloons.
Choices A and C are incorrect because we know the people who participate are part of Krewes. People who work the floats and parades are also part of Krewes

Choice D is incorrect because the passage makes no mention of people who do not celebrate Mardi Gras.

28. A

Helen's parents hired Anne to teach Helen to communicate. Choice B is incorrect because the passage states Anne had trouble finding her way around, which means she could walk. Choice C is incorrect because you don't hire a teacher to teach someone to play. Choice D is incorrect because by age 6, if Helen had never eaten, she would have starved to death.

29. B
The correct answer because that fact is stated directly in the passage. The passage explains that Anne taught Helen to hear by allowing her to feel the vibrations in her throat.

30. A
We can infer that Anne is a patient teacher because she did not leave or lose her temper when Helen bit or hit her; she just kept trying to teach Helen. Choice B is incorrect because Anne taught Helen to read and talk. Choice C is incorrect because Anne could hear. She was partially blind, not deaf. Choice D is incorrect because it does not have to do with patience.

Listening Comprehension

1. B
Household fires are so common because we use fire so often.

2. A
Most fires start in the kitchen.

3. B
Another major cause of fires is smoking.

4. C
The owners, Mary and John Smith went downtown for the day. Choice D is not mentioned at all, and can be eliminated right away. Choice B, visiting their friend upstairs, and choice C, are meant to confuse – the neighbor upstairs is mentioned in the news story, as the person that called them, but they were downtown at the time. Choices C is incorrect – the news story does mention they had breakfast, but it was not the cause of the fire.

5. A
Choice A, a candle left burning near some papers on a bookshelf is the correct answer. Choice B can be eliminated right away as it is not mentioned at all. The other choices, C and D are intended to distract. The neighbor and breakfast are mentioned, but not as the cause of the fire.

6. A

Yes their home burned down completely. From the story, "When Mary and John got home, the fire department had put out the fire, and there was only ashes."

7. B

Tom was going to school when he noticed the burning house.

8. B

Tom called the emergency services when he saw the house was on fire. From the passage, ". The teenager immediately called the emergency service and gave the address."

9. C

It took a long time for the fire department to arrive because the house was out of time

10. A

Most volcanoes are underwater

11. B

A split in the earth's plates causes volcanoes.

12. A

The volcano Vesuvius covered the city of Pompeii in minutes.

13. C

Shield volcanoes are common in the Hawaiian volcanic chain

14. B

Stratovolcanoes, which are tall conical mountains formed of lava flows

15. B

Underwater volcanoes do not have big explosions due to the weight of the water.

Mathematics

1. D
8327 − 1278 = 7049

2. B
294 X 21 = 6174

3. C
1278 + 4920 = 6198

4. A
285 * 12 = 3420

5. C
4120 − 3216 = 904

6. D
2417 + 1004 = 3421

7. B
1440 ÷ 12 = 120

8. C
2713 − 1308 = 1405

9. B
Formula for perimeter of a rectangle is 2(L + W)
The perimeter, p = 26, so 2(L+W) = p

The length is 5 inches more than the width, so

2(w+5) + 2w = 26
2w + 10 + 2w = 26
2w + 2w = 26 - 10
4w = 16

W = 16/4 = 4 inches

L is 5 inches more than w, so L = 5 + 4 = 9 inches.

10. B
Let the father's age = Y, and Kate's age = X, therefore
Y = 32 + X, in 5 yrs y = 5x, substituting for Y will be
5x = 32 + X, 5x − x = 32, 4X = 32, X = 32/8, x = 8,
Kate will be 8 in 5 yrs time, so Kate's present age = 8 - 5 = 3.

11. D
Total cost of the items is $21,045 + $3,905 + $1,450 = $26,400
Total cost is now $26,400 + $5000 profit = $31,400

12. A
Number of mangos in the basket is 3/5 x 125 = 75
Number of ripe mangos = 2/5 x 75 = 30

13. D
The cost of the dishwasher = $450
15% discount amount = (450 * 15)/100 = $67.5
The discounted price = 450 − 67.5 = $382.5
20% additional discount amount on lowest price = (382.5 * 20)/100 = $76.5
So, the final discounted price = 382.5 - 76.5 = $306.00

14. D
Original price = x,
80/100 = 12590/X,
80X = 1259000,
X = 15737.50.

15. C
Total hay = 214 kg,
The goat eats at a rate of 214/60 days = 3.6 kg per day.
The Cow eats at a rate of 214/15 = 14.3 kg per day,
Together they eat 3.6 + 14.3 = 17.9 per day.
At a rate of 17.9 kg per day, they will consume 214 kg in 214/17.9 = 11.96 or about 12 days.

16. A
25% = 25/100 = 1/4

17. C
125/100 = 1.25

18. D
40/100 = 30/X = 40X = 30*100 = 3000/40 = 75

19. B
12.5/100 = 50/X = 12.5X = 50 * 100 = 5000/12.5 = 400

20. C
24/56 = 3/7 (divide numerator and denominator by 8)

21. C
Converting percent to decimal – divide percent by 100 and remove the % sign. 87% = 87/100 = .87

22. A
60 has the same relation to X as 75 to 100 – so
60/X = 75/100
6000 = 75X
X = 80

23. D
60 has the same relationship to 100 as 12 does to X – so
60/100 = 12/X
1200 = 60X
X = 20

24. C
Converting a fraction to a decimal – divide the numerator by the denominator – so 71/1000 = .071. Dividing by 1000 moves the decimal point 3 places.

25. C
4.7 + .9 + .01 = 5.61

26. D
.84 ÷ .7 = 1.2

27. C
9 is in the ten thousandths place in 1.7389.

28. A
.87 - .48 = .39

29. C
1 foot = 12 inches, 60 feet = 60 x 12 = 720 inches.

30. A
1 centimeter = 10 millimeter, 25 centimeter = 25 X 10 = 250.

Mechanical Aptitude

1. B
The smaller the distance between threads, the easier to turn.

2. C
75 pounds of force much be exerted downward on the rope to lift the 150 pound weight.

3. B
To solve for F, Weight X b (distance from fulcrum to weight) = Force X a (distance from fulcrum to point where force is applied)
100 X 5 = F X 10
500/10 = F
F = 50

4. B
First calculate the speed of gear B. The gear ratio is 10:40 or 1:4. If gear A is turning at 80 rpm, then gear B, which is larger, will turn slower, 80/4 = 20 rpm.

Next calculate B and C. Gear C is smaller, so it will turn faster. The gear ratio is 40:10 or 4:1, and since gear B turns at 20 rpm, gear C will turn at 20 X 4 = 80 rpm.

Next calculate the direction. Gear A is turning clockwise, so Gear B is turning counter clockwise, so Gear C must be turning clockwise.

5. C
Notice the weight is attached to two of the pulleys. The weight required will therefore be 100/4 = 25 pounds.

6. B
A cam is a rotating or sliding piece in a mechanical linkage used especially in transforming rotary motion into linear motion or vice-versa

7. A
The function of the crankshaft is to transform the back-and-forth motion of the pistons into rotary motion.

8. B
The smaller gear will travel twice as fast as the larger gear.

9. A
A tachometer (revolution-counter, Tach, rev-counter, RPM gauge) is an instrument measuring the rotation speed of a shaft or disk, as in a motor or other machine. The device usually displays the revolutions per minute (RPM) on a calibrated analogue dial, but digital displays are increasingly common. [16]

10. B
A hex key, Allen key, or Allen wrench (also known by various other synonyms) is a tool of hexagonal cross-section (6-sided) used to drive bolts and screws that have a hexagonal socket in the head (internal-wrenching hexagon drive). [18]

11. A
A chuck is used to tighten bits in an electric drill.

12. C
There are three hydrants on Los Felix Blvd.

13. A
Taking the shortest route from Golden State Fwy 5 and Los Felix, to Santa Monica Blvd and Versont, there is one corner.

14. B
The width of the house from west to east is 37 feet.

15. C
The length of the house from north to south is 46 feet.

16. A
Choice B has the garage on the opposite side. Choice C does not have the indented front window beside the garage. Choice D has the front of the garage even with the front of the house.
17. A
Choice B is an entirely different house. Choice C is a different house the front porch extending out the front instead of inset. Choice D is the same house flipped horizontally.

18. B
The greater the distance over which the force is applied, the smaller the force required (to lift the load).

19. C
The block and tackle system composed of a system of pulleys as shown operates according the following rule:

Pulling Force = Load / (Number of supporting ropes)

Here Load and Weight are the same thing.

Here, the number of supporting ropes is 4. So, we have

F = 360/4

Force = 90 N Choice C

Feedback for Choice D

Do not confuse the number of supporting ropes. The rope which is being pulled is not counted. Otherwise, you will obtain the wrong answer choice D 72 (360 / 5).

20. D
The equation of meshed gears states that the speed of rotation V (in rot/s) is inversely proportional to the number of teeth N. Mathematically,

$$N_1 \cdot V_1 = N_2 \cdot V_2 = N_3 \cdot V_3$$

Here, we are concerned only for the gears 1 and 3. Thus, we have
$7 \cdot V_1 = 30 \cdot 210$
$V_1 = (30 \cdot 210)/7 = 900$ turns

Mapping

1. B
The fastest route is A12 – A8 – A6 – A5 which takes 14 minutes. To return, A5 – A7 – A10 – A11 – A12 takes 23 minutes. Total time is 37 minutes.

2. D
The route to R is, N – P – Q – R which takes 11 minutes. The route back, avoiding O, is R – X – W – V which takes 14 minutes. Total time is 25 minutes.

3. A
The fastest route is A18 – A8 – A7 – V – N – V – A7 – A8 – A18. Total time is 41 minutes.

4. C
The fastest route is A3 – A5 – A7 – A10, which takes 12 minutes. 30 seconds stop at A5 and A7 is one minute. From A10 - A9 – W takes 7 minutes. Total time is 20 minutes.

5. A
The fastest route from U to A4 through V, is U – V – A7 – A8 – A6 – A4 and it takes 15 minutes. The car makes a turn at V and A8, that is 30 seconds. Total is 15 minutes, 30 seconds.

6. B
The fastest route is F – E – D – C – B – A. The first 2 blocks by car will take 7 minutes. The next 2 blocks by bike will take 10 minutes, the last block on foot would take 10 minutes. Total time 27 minutes.

7. D
The fastest route is R – X – A11 – A10 and it takes 7 minutes by car. He makes a turn at A11 for 30 seconds. Total time is 7 minutes, 30 seconds.

8. A
The fastest route is V – A7 – A8 – A18. By bike would take 15 minutes. From A18 through A16 to A14 by car would go through A18 – A17 – A16 – A4. By car would take 10 minutes. Total time is 25 minutes.

9. C

The shortest route is S – H – J – I – L – M – K. By bike it would take 23 minutes.

10. D

From D to V by bike would take 16 minutes. Walking from O to W would take 16 minutes. From B to A3 by car would take 16 minutes. So all three routes would take same time.

11. D

The fastest route that goes through V and A6 is U – V – A7 – A8 – A6 – A17 – A18. By bike would take 31 minutes.

12. B

The fastest route is U – A5 – A6 – A8. By car it would take 11 minutes. Then on foot to A12 would take 6 minutes. Total time is 17 minutes.

13. A

Fastest route is T – A1 – A2 – A4 – A16 – A15. Time on foot is 38 minutes.

14. D

Best route is S – T – U – V – W in 13 minutes.

15. C

The fastest route is G – I – L – N – O, which would take 20 minutes by bike.

Situation Judgment

1. B

Building relationships involves being approachable and supportive. Offering help fosters a positive and collaborative team environment.

2. B

Effective teamwork requires open communication and willingness to find common ground. Discussing and compromising ensures that both perspectives are considered.

3. B
Building relationships and being a team player involves being receptive to feedback and making adjustments to improve team dynamics.

4. A
Introducing incentives is likely to motivate your team members. Choice B, reducing compensation is likely to alienating. Choice C, talking about the need to be committed could easily come across as talking down. Choice D, is not realistic.

While compensating the employees who perform exemplary, one creates unnecessary competition zones which could in turn be bad for business.

5. A
It's important to make your side of the story known as a way to avoid confusion and misinterpretation.

By blaming and accusing others you don't help yourself.

6. A
The first step in dealing with difficult people is to stay calm and understand their point of view.

After that you can start to build rapport.

Choice C, reporting to your supervisor you can't work with them may be a second step but basically doesn't solve the problem. Choice D, ignoring their unhelpful behavior, depends on how serious it is – if it is minor this may be OK.

However, Choice A, is the best choice because you are going to have to get along with them.

7. D
The best thing with failure is the lessons it brings. By encouraging him or her to learn from their mistakes, you give them the chance to improve.

Choice A, criticizing does nothing to improving their situation. The person criticized will in turn find fault in you and blame you. Focus on the issues that bring success to the business.

8. A
It is important therefore to refer your colleague to a guidance session where he can get the appropriate assistance.

Comparing their problems with yours, Choice B, will not make them feel any better or be able to perform better. Reporting this matter to the supervisor, choice C, could solve the problem, but also could bring problems to your colleague and worsen their condition. Unless you have been trained on how to handle stress-related issues, then it's not advisable to give counseling sessions to a person who shows signs of distress. It could accomplish quite the opposite.

9. A
This will help the colleague understand the importance of respecting protocol.

10. D
This will help the intern know what to concentrate on in their future reports.

The other choices, A, B and C do offer long-term solutions.

11. B
this will save everyone's time as the entire team is paying little attention to the presentation.
The other choices, A, C and D do not provide solutions that will benefit the entire team.

12. D
It is the responsibility of the employee to inform their manager of their intention to leave. This will help the manager in planning for the future. It will also give the manager a chance to address issues that might have caused you to look elsewhere for employment. It is also important to continue working normally as you are still an employee of the company you work for.

13. B

By choosing choice B you will show honesty and genuine interest in the issue at hand. This serves the purpose of educating your co-worker on the benefits of cooperation. It is fair to take more action if the co-worker chooses to ignore your advice.

14. D

A joint project requires teamwork and team work requires communication and constant negotiation on what should be done and how it should be done. Negotiating and distributing the work fairly between the two of you will ensure he steps up and takes responsibility for his part of the project. However, because of the situation and poor performance will reflect badly on you as well, be prepared to put in some extra.

15. D

A colleague will be able to sort out the customer's problem.

AFTER TAKING A PRACTICE TEST

What to do after you take a practice test

Go through your answers carefully. For each wrong answer, refer to the explanation, and work through the questions step-by-step.

What kind of question (e.g. reading comprehension, science, algebra, basic math etc.)

Look for patterns in your incorrect answers – what is it exactly that you are doing wrong or don't understand. What types of questions do you have the most difficulty with? Refer to the tutorials and try to understand the questions.

Getting the Most from Practice Questions

Taking a practice test is probably the best way to prepare for a test.

Quick tips to get the most from practice questions:

Simulate Test Conditions

- Choose a quiet, distraction-free environment.

- Use a timer and allow just under 1 minute per question.

- Avoid using notes or online texts

Take it seriously -

- Treat the practice test as if it's the real exam -

- Familiarize yourself with the format and topics - this will reduce anxiety.

After Completing a Practice Test

Reviewing your work after you take a practice test is critical.

Immediate Review

- Make a note of any questions you found challenging or topics that felt unfamiliar or difficult.

- How was your time management?

- Overall comfort during the test?

Do a Thorough Review

- Go over your answers focusing on correct and incorrect answers.

- For incorrect answers, identify misunderstandings knowledge gaps or problem subject areas - here is where you need to spend your study time.

Look for Patterns

- Look for recurring themes in your errors to pinpoint specific areas needing improvement.

- Assess whether mistakes were due to content gaps, misinterpretation of questions, or time constraints.

Physical Fitness Requirements and Test

Firefighters in Canada are required to be in good physical condition, as the job can be physically demanding.

Below is a general guide to physical requirements and some examples. Most fire departments require applicants to complete a physical fitness test.

Physical fitness: Firefighting is physically demanding work and firefighters must be physically fit to perform day-to-day tasks such as carrying heavy equipment, climbing stairs, crawling through small spaces, lifting and carrying heavy objects, such as hoses, ladders, and rescue equipment.

Firefighters often work for extended periods in physically demanding conditions, requiring strength and stamina.

Coordination, Vision and Hearing: Firefighters require excellent hand-to-eye coordination, hearing and visual acuity.

Some fire departments have a vision test as part of the hiring process.

Example Physical tasks in a Fitness test:

- Navigate in a Confined Space
- Ladder Climb
- Drag an 80 kb Sled 30 meters
- Extend a ladder vertically 10.67M (35') to the

maximum extension
- Carry a hose or other heavy object 5 stories twice
- Lift hose roll weighing 25kg (55lb) and carry to a height of 17m
- Carry a hydrant kit in one hand and walk across the rungs of a 4.2m (14') ladder without falling off the ladder
- Advance 45m (150') of charged 45mm (1¾") fire hose 30m (100').
- Lift and carry a 41kg (90lb) roll of large diameter supply line 15m (50').

Requirements vary depending on the specific fire department you are applying to. Some departments may have additional requirements and some are more stringent than others.

Conclusion

CONGRATULATIONS! You have made it this far because you have applied yourself diligently to practicing for the exam and no doubt improved your potential score considerably! Getting into a good school is a huge step in a journey that might be challenging at times but will be many times more rewarding and fulfilling. That is why being prepared is so important.

Study then Practice and then Succeed!

Good Luck!

Register for Free Updates and More Practice Test Questions

Register your purchase at
https://www.test-preparation.ca/register/

for updates, free test tips and more practice test questions.

Feedback

We welcome your feedback. Email us at feedback@test-preparation.ca with your comments and suggestions. We carefully review all suggestions and often incorporate reader suggestions into upcoming versions. As a Print on Demand Publisher, we update our products frequently.

https://www.facebook.com/CompleteTestPreparation/

https://www.youtube.com/user/MrTestPreparation

ONLINE RESOURCES

How to Prepare for a Test - The Ultimate Guide

https://www.test-preparation.ca/prepare-test/

Learning Styles - The Complete Guide

https://www.test-preparation.ca/learning-style/

Test Anxiety Secrets!

https://www.test-preparation.ca/test-anxiety/

Time Management on a Test

https://www.test-preparation.ca/time-management/

Flash Cards - The Complete Guide

https://www.test-preparation.ca/flash-cards/

Test Preparation Video Series

https://www.test-preparation.ca/test-video/

How to Memorize - The Complete Guide

https://www.test-preparation.ca/memorize/

Online Library of Student Tips and Strategies

https://www.test-preparation.ca/students-say/

www.ingramcontent.com/pod-product-compliance
Lightning Source LLC
Chambersburg PA
CBHW072148070526
44585CB00015B/1050